Just The

Textbook Key Facts

Textbook Outlines, Highlights, and Practice Quizzes

Managerial Economics

by Luke M. Froeb, 3rd Edition

All "Just the Facts101" Material Written or Prepared by Cram101 Textbook Reviews

Title Page

STUDYING MADE EASY

This Facts101 notebook is designed to make studying easier and increase your comprehension of the textbook material. Instead of starting with a blank notebook and trying to write down everything discussed in class lectures, you can use this Facts101 textbook notebook and annotate your notes along with the lecture.

Our goal is to give you the best tools for success.

For a supreme understanding of the course, pair your notebook with our online tools. Should you decide you prefer jtf101.com as your study tool,

we'd like to offer you a trade...

Our Trade In program is a simple way for us to keep our promise and provide you the best studying tools, regardless of where you purchased your Facts101 textbook notebook. As long as your notebook is in *Like New Condition**, you can send it back to us and we will immediately give you a JustTheFacts101.com account free for 120 days!

Let The *Trade In* Begin!

THREE SIMPLE STEPS TO TRADE:

1. Go to www.jtf101.com/tradein and fill out the packing slip information.

2. Submit and print the packing slip and mail it in with your Facts101 textbook notebook.

3. Activate your account after you receive your email confirmation.

* Books must be returned in *Like New Condition*, meaning there is no damage to the book including, but not limited to; ripped or torn pages, markings or writing on pages, or folded / creased pages. Upon receiving the book, Facts101 will inspect it and reserves the right to terminate your free Facts101.com account and return your textbook notebook at the owners expense.

LEARNING SYSTEM

"Just the Facts101" is a Content Technologies publication and tool designed to give you all the facts from your textbooks. Visit JustTheFacts101.com for the full practice test for each of your chapters for virtually any of your textbooks.

Facts101 has built custom study tools specific to your textbook. We provide all of the factual testable information and unlike traditional study guides, we will never send you back to your textbook for more information.

YOU WILL NEVER HAVE TO HIGHLIGHT A BOOK AGAIN!

Facts101 StudyGuides

All of the information in this StudyGuide is written specifically for your textbook. We include the key terms, places, people, and concepts... the information you can expect on your next exam!

Want to take a practice test?

Throughout each chapter of this StudyGuide you will find links to JustTheFacts101.com where you can select specific chapters to take a complete test on, or you can subscribe and get practice tests for up to 12 of your textbooks, along with other exclusive Jtf101.com tools like problem solving labs and reference libraries.

JustTheFacts101.com

Only Jtf101.com gives you the outlines, highlights, and PRACTICE TESTS specific to your textbook. JustTheFacts101.com is an online application where you'll discover study tools designed to make the most of your limited study time.

By purchasing this book, you get 50% off the normal monthly subscription fee!. Just enter the promotional code **'DK73DW30063'** on the Jtf101.com registration screen.

www.JustTheFacts101.com

Managerial Economics
Luke M. Froeb, 3rd

CONTENTS

1. Introduction: What This Book Is About

CHAPTER OUTLINE: KEY TERMS, PEOPLE, PLACES, CONCEPTS

	Prisoner's dilemma
	Economics
	Marginal cost
	Economic profit
	Consequentialist
	Enron
	Goldman Sachs
	Job interview
	Interview
	Internet
	Adverse selection

CHAPTER HIGHLIGHTS & NOTES: KEY TERMS, PEOPLE, PLACES, CONCEPTS

Prisoner's dilemma	The prisoner's dilemma is a canonical example of a game analyzed in game theory that shows why two purely 'rational' individuals might not cooperate, even if it appears that it is in their best interests to do so. It was originally framed by Merrill Flood and Melvin Dresher working at RAND in 1950. Albert W. Tucker formalized the game with prison sentence rewards and gave it the name 'prisoner's dilemma' (Poundstone, 1992), presenting it as follows:Two members of a criminal gang are arrested and imprisoned. Each prisoner is in solitary confinement with no means of speaking to or exchanging messages with the other.
Economics	Economics is the social science that studies the behavior of individuals, groups, and organizations, when they manage or use scarce resources, which have alternative uses, to achieve desired ends. Agents are assumed to act rationally, have multiple desirable ends in sight, limited resources to obtain these ends, a set of stable preferences, a definite overall guiding objective, and the capability of making a choice.

1. Introduction: What This Book Is About

Marginal cost	In economics and finance, marginal cost is the change in the total cost that arises when the quantity produced has an increment by unit. That is, it is the cost of producing one more unit of a good. In general terms, marginal cost at each level of production includes any additional costs required to produce the next unit.
Economic profit	In neoclassical microeconomic theory, the term profit has two related but distinct meanings. Economic profit is similar to accounting profit but smaller because it reflects the total opportunity costs (both explicit and implicit) of a venture to an investor. Normal profit refers to a situation in which the economic profit is zero.
Consequentialist	Consequentialism is the class of normative ethical theories holding that the consequences of one's conduct are the ultimate basis for any judgment about the rightness or wrongness of that conduct. Thus, from a consequentialist standpoint, a morally right act (or omission from acting) is one that will produce a good outcome, or consequence. In an extreme form, the idea of consequentialism is commonly encapsulated in the English saying, 'the ends justify the means', meaning that if a goal is morally important enough, any method of achieving it is acceptable.
Enron	Enron Corporation was an American energy, commodities, and services company based in Houston, Texas. Before its bankruptcy on December 2, 2001, Enron employed approximately 20,000 staff and was one of the world's major electricity, natural gas, communications, and pulp and paper companies, with claimed revenues of nearly $101 billion during 2000. Fortune named Enron 'America's Most Innovative Company' for six consecutive years. At the end of 2001, it was revealed that its reported financial condition was sustained substantially by an institutionalized, systematic, and creatively planned accounting fraud, known since as the Enron scandal.
Goldman Sachs	The Goldman Sachs Group, Inc. is an American multinational investment banking firm that engages in global investment banking, securities, investment management, and other financial services primarily with institutional clients. Goldman Sachs was founded in 1869 and is headquartered at 200 West Street in the Lower Manhattan area of New York City, with additional offices in international financial centers.
Job interview	A job interview is a type of employment test that involves a conversation between a job applicant and representative of the employing organization. Interviews are one of the most popularly used devices for employee selection. Interviews vary in the extent to which the questions are structured, from totally unstructured and free-wheeling conversation, to a set list of questions each applicant is asked.
Interview	An interview is a conversation between two or more people where questions are asked by the interviewer to elicit facts or statements from the interviewee.

	Interviews are a standard part of journalism and media reporting, but are also employed in many other situations, including qualitative research.
Internet	The Internet is a global system of interconnected computer networks that use the standard Internet protocol suite to link several billion devices worldwide. It is a network of networks that consists of millions of private, public, academic, business, and government networks, of local to global scope, that are linked by a broad array of electronic, wireless, and optical networking technologies. The Internet carries an extensive range of information resources and services, such as the inter-linked hypertext documents and applications of the World Wide Web (WWW), the infrastructure to support email, and peer-to-peer networks for file sharing and telephony.
Adverse selection	Adverse selection, anti-selection, or negative selection is a term used in economics, insurance, risk management, and statistics. It refers to a market process in which undesired results occur when buyers and sellers have asymmetric information (access to different information); the 'bad' products or services are more likely to be selected. For example, a bank that sets one price for all of its checking account customers runs the risk of being adversely selected against by its low-balance, high-activity (and hence least profitable) customers.

1. The _____ is a canonical example of a game analyzed in game theory that shows why two purely 'rational' individuals might not cooperate, even if it appears that it is in their best interests to do so. It was originally framed by Merrill Flood and Melvin Dresher working at RAND in 1950. Albert W. Tucker formalized the game with prison sentence rewards and gave it the name '_____' (Poundstone, 1992), presenting it as follows: Two members of a criminal gang are arrested and imprisoned. Each prisoner is in solitary confinement with no means of speaking to or exchanging messages with the other.

    a. Gresham's Law
    b. Spindletop
    c. Prisoner's dilemma
    d. Libya

2. . _____ is the social science that studies the behavior of individuals, groups, and organizations, when they manage or use scarce resources, which have alternative uses, to achieve desired ends. Agents are assumed to act rationally, have multiple desirable ends in sight, limited resources to obtain these ends, a set of stable preferences, a definite overall guiding objective, and the capability of making a choice. There exists an _____(s) problem, subject to study by _____(s) science, when a decision (choice) has to be made by one or more resource-controlling players to attain the best possible outcome under bounded rational conditions.

1. Introduction: What This Book Is About

a. Associative economics
b. Easterlin hypothesis
c. Economics
d. Identity economics

3. In economics and finance, _____ is the change in the total cost that arises when the quantity produced has an increment by unit. That is, it is the cost of producing one more unit of a good. In general terms, _____ at each level of production includes any additional costs required to produce the next unit.

a. Benefit principle
b. Marginal cost
c. Club good
d. Conjectural variation

4. An _____ is a conversation between two or more people where questions are asked by the interviewer to elicit facts or statements from the interviewee. _____s are a standard part of journalism and media reporting, but are also employed in many other situations, including qualitative research.

a. Interview
b. Group concept mapping
c. Box social
d. Bid-to-cover ratio

5. _____ Corporation was an American energy, commodities, and services company based in Houston, Texas. Before its bankruptcy on December 2, 2001, _____ employed approximately 20,000 staff and was one of the world's major electricity, natural gas, communications, and pulp and paper companies, with claimed revenues of nearly $101 billion during 2000. Fortune named _____ 'America's Most Innovative Company' for six consecutive years.

At the end of 2001, it was revealed that its reported financial condition was sustained substantially by an institutionalized, systematic, and creatively planned accounting fraud, known since as the _____ scandal.

a. Enron
b. Bank fraud
c. Bear raid
d. Bill and hold

1. c

2. c

3. b

4. a

5. a

You can take the complete Chapter Practice Test

for 1. Introduction: What This Book Is About
on all key terms, persons, places, and concepts.

Online 99 Cents

http://www.JustTheFacts101.com

Use www.JustTheFacts101.com for all your study needs

including Facts101's online interactive problem solving labs in

chemistry, statistics, mathematics, and more.

2. The One Lesson of Business

CHAPTER OUTLINE: KEY TERMS, PEOPLE, PLACES, CONCEPTS

_____ | Gains from trade

_____ | Value

_____ | Capitalism

_____ | Property rights

_____ | Economic profit

_____ | Efficiency

_____ | Henry

_____ | Subsidies

_____ | Taxes

_____ | Economics

_____ | Price ceiling

_____ | Price floor

_____ | Control

_____ | Price controls

2. The One Lesson of Business

Gains from trade	In economics, gains from trade refers to net benefits to agents from allowing an increase in voluntary trading with each other. In technical terms, it is the increase of consumer surplus plus producer surplus from lower tariffs or otherwise liberalizing trade.
Value	Economic value is a measure of the benefit that an economic actor can gain from either a good or service. It is generally measured relative to units of currency, and the interpretation is therefore 'what is the maximum amount of money a specific actor is willing and able to pay for the good or service'?
	Note that economic value is not the same as market price. If a consumer is willing to buy a good, it implies that the customer places a higher value on the good than the market price.
Capitalism	Capitalism is an economic system in which trade, industry and the means of production are controlled by private owners with the goal of making profits in a market economy. Central characteristics of capitalism include capital accumulation, competitive markets and wage labor. In a capitalist economy, the parties to a transaction typically determine the prices at which assets, goods, and services are exchanged.
Property rights	Property rights are theoretical constructs in economics for determining how a resource is used and owned. Resources can be owned (the subject of property) by individuals, associations or governments. Property rights can be viewed as an attribute of an economic good.
Economic profit	In neoclassical microeconomic theory, the term profit has two related but distinct meanings. Economic profit is similar to accounting profit but smaller because it reflects the total opportunity costs (both explicit and implicit) of a venture to an investor. Normal profit refers to a situation in which the economic profit is zero.
Efficiency	The relative efficiency of two procedures is the ratio of their efficiencies, although often this term is used where the comparison is made between a given procedure and a notional 'best possible' procedure. The efficiencies and the relative efficiency of two procedures theoretically depend on the sample size available for the given procedure, but it is often possible to use the asymptotic relative efficiency as the principal comparison measure.
	Efficiencies are often defined using the variance or mean square error as the measure of desirability.
Henry	Henry was an Obotrite prince or king (1093-1127) from the Nakonid dynasty; he was regarded by contemporaries as 'King of the Slavs' (rex Slavorum). The Obotrite realm reached its greatest area during Henry's rule, extending from the Elbe to the Oder and from the Havelland to the Baltic Sea.

2. The One Lesson of Business

Subsidies	A subsidy is a form of financial or in kind support extended to an economic sector generally with the aim of promoting economic and social policy. Although commonly extended from Government, the term subsidy can relate to any type of support - for example from NGOs or implicit subsidies. Subsidies come in various forms including: direct (cash grants, interest-free loans) and indirect (tax breaks, insurance, low-interest loans, depreciation write-offs, rent rebates).
Taxes	A tax is a financial charge or other levy imposed upon a taxpayer (an individual or legal entity) by a state or the functional equivalent of a state such that failure to pay is punishable by law. Taxes are also imposed by many administrative divisions. Taxes consist of direct or indirect taxes and may be paid in money or as its labour equivalent.
Economics	Economics is the social science that studies the behavior of individuals, groups, and organizations, when they manage or use scarce resources, which have alternative uses, to achieve desired ends. Agents are assumed to act rationally, have multiple desirable ends in sight, limited resources to obtain these ends, a set of stable preferences, a definite overall guiding objective, and the capability of making a choice. There exists an economic problem, subject to study by economic science, when a decision (choice) has to be made by one or more resource-controlling players to attain the best possible outcome under bounded rational conditions.
Price ceiling	A price ceiling is a government-imposed price control or limit on how high a price is charged for a product. Governments intend price ceilings to protect consumers from conditions that could make necessary commodities unattainable. However, a price ceiling can cause problems if imposed for a long period without controlled rationing.
Price floor	A price floor is a government- or group-imposed price control or limit on how low a price can be charged for a product. A price floor must be greater than the equilibrium price in order to be effective.
Control	Controlling is one of the managerial functions like planning, organizing, staffing and directing. It is an important function because it helps to check the errors and to take the corrective action so that deviation from standards are minimized and stated goals of the organization are achieved in a desired manner. According to modern concepts, control is a foreseeing action whereas earlier concept of control was used only when errors were detected.
Price controls	Price controls are governmental restrictions on the prices that can be charged for goods and services in a market. The intent behind implementing such controls can stem from the desire to maintain affordability of staple foods and goods, to prevent price gouging during shortages, and to slow inflation, or, alternatively, to insure a minimum income for providers of certain goods or a minimum wage.

2. The One Lesson of Business

1. In economics, _____ refers to net benefits to agents from allowing an increase in voluntary trading with each other. In technical terms, it is the increase of consumer surplus plus producer surplus from lower tariffs or otherwise liberalizing trade.

   a. 2008 G-20 Washington summit
   b. Backsourcing
   c. Gains from trade
   d. Brazilian disease

2. _____ is an economic system in which trade, industry and the means of production are controlled by private owners with the goal of making profits in a market economy. Central characteristics of _____ include capital accumulation, competitive markets and wage labor. In a capitalist economy, the parties to a transaction typically determine the prices at which assets, goods, and services are exchanged.

   a. Cigar Box Method
   b. Cash crop
   c. Capitalism
   d. CAPRI model

3. Economic _____ is a measure of the benefit that an economic actor can gain from either a good or service. It is generally measured relative to units of currency, and the interpretation is therefore 'what is the maximum amount of money a specific actor is willing and able to pay for the good or service'?

   Note that economic _____ is not the same as market price. If a consumer is willing to buy a good, it implies that the customer places a higher _____ on the good than the market price.

   a. Benefit principle
   b. Value
   c. Club good
   d. Conjectural variation

4. A _____ is a government-imposed price control or limit on how high a price is charged for a product. Governments intend _____s to protect consumers from conditions that could make necessary commodities unattainable. However, a _____ can cause problems if imposed for a long period without controlled rationing.

   a. Flour War
   b. Price ceiling
   c. Price support
   d. Socialist accumulation

5. . _____ are theoretical constructs in economics for determining how a resource is used and owned. Resources can be owned (the subject of property) by individuals, associations or governments. _____ can be viewed as an attribute of an economic good.

   a. Common ownership

b. Common-pool resource
c. Counter-mapping
d. Property rights

1. c
2. c
3. b
4. b
5. d

You can take the complete Chapter Practice Test

for 2. The One Lesson of Business
on all key terms, persons, places, and concepts.

Online 99 Cents

http://www.JustTheFacts101.com

Use www.JustTheFacts101.com for all your study needs

including Facts101's online interactive problem solving labs in

chemistry, statistics, mathematics, and more.

3. Benefits, Costs, and Decisions

CHAPTER OUTLINE: KEY TERMS, PEOPLE, PLACES, CONCEPTS

	Average cost
	Cost curve
	Capital cost
	Fixed cost
	Total cost
	Capital
	Variable
	Variable cost
	Economic value
	Economic Value Added
	Economic profit
	Economic cost
	Expense
	Implicit cost
	Explicit cost
	Opportunity cost
	Cost
	Depreciation
	Overhead
	Selling
	Generally accepted accounting principles

3. Benefits, Costs, and Decisions

	Lehman Brothers
	Subprime mortgage crisis

Average cost	In economics, average cost or unit cost is equal to total cost divided by the number of goods produced . It is also equal to the sum of average variable costs (total variable costs divided by Q) plus average fixed costs (total fixed costs divided by Q). Average costs may be dependent on the time period considered (increasing production may be expensive or impossible in the short term, for example).
Cost curve	In economics, a cost curve is a graph of the costs of production as a function of total quantity produced. In a free market economy, productively efficient firms use these curves to find the optimal point of production (minimizing cost), and profit maximizing firms can use them to decide output quantities to achieve those aims. There are various types of cost curves, all related to each other, including total and average cost curves, and marginal ('for each additional unit') cost curves, which are equal to the differential of the total cost curves.
Capital cost	Capital costs are fixed, one-time expenses incurred on the purchase of land, buildings, construction, and equipment used in the production of goods or in the rendering of services. Put simply, it is the total cost needed to bring a project to a commercially operable status. Whether a particular cost is capital or not depend on many factors such as accounting, tax laws, and materiality.
Fixed cost	In economics, fixed costs, indirect costs or overheads are business expenses that are not dependent on the level of goods or services produced by the business. They tend to be time-related, such as salaries or rents being paid per month, and are often referred to as overhead costs. This is in contrast to variable costs, which are volume-related (and are paid per quantity produced).
Total cost	In economics, and cost accounting, total cost describes the total economic cost of production and is made up of variable costs, which vary according to the quantity of a good produced and include inputs such as labor and raw materials, plus fixed costs, which are independent of the quantity of a good produced and include inputs (capital) that cannot be varied in the short term, such as buildings and machinery. Total cost in economics includes the total opportunity cost of each factor of production as part of its fixed or variable costs.

Capital	In economics, capital goods, real capital, or capital assets are already-produced durable goods or any non-financial asset that is used in production of goods or services.
	Capital goods are not significantly consumed in the production process though they may depreciate. How a capital good or is maintained or returned to its pre-production state varies with the type of capital involved.
Variable	In elementary mathematics, a variable is an alphabetic character representing a number which is either arbitrary or not fully specified or unknown. Making algebraic computations with variables as if they were explicit numbers allows one to solve a range of problems in a single computation. A typical example is the quadratic formula, which allows to solve every quadratic equation by simply substituting the numeric values of the coefficients of the given equation to the variables that represent them.
Variable cost	Variable costs are costs that change in proportion to the good or service that a business produces. Variable costs are also the sum of marginal costs over all units produced. They can also be considered normal costs.
Economic value	Economic value is a measure of the benefit provided by a good or service to an economic agent. It is generally measured relative to units of currency, and the interpretation is therefore 'what is the maximum amount of money a specific actor is willing and able to pay for the good or service'?
	Note that economic value is not the same as market price. If a consumer is willing to buy a good, it implies that the customer places a higher value on the good than the market price.
Economic Value Added	In corporate finance, Economic Value Added, is an estimate of a firm's economic profit - being the value created in excess of the required return of the company's investors (being shareholders and debt holders). Quite simply, Economic Value Added is the profit earned by the firm less the cost of financing the firm's capital. The idea is that value is created when the return on the firm's economic capital employed is greater than the cost of that capital.
Economic profit	In neoclassical microeconomic theory, the term profit has two related but distinct meanings. Economic profit is similar to accounting profit but smaller because it reflects the total opportunity costs (both explicit and implicit) of a venture to an investor. Normal profit refers to a situation in which the economic profit is zero.
Economic cost	The economic cost of a decision depends on both the cost of the alternative chosen and the benefit that the best alternative would have provided if chosen. Economic cost differs from accounting cost because it includes opportunity cost.
	As an example, consider the economic cost of attending college.

3. Benefits, Costs, and Decisions

Expense	In common usage, an expense or expenditure is an outflow of money to another person or group to pay for an item or service, or for a category of costs. For a tenant, rent is an expense. For students or parents, tuition is an expense.
Implicit cost	In economics, an implicit cost, also called an imputed cost, implied cost, or notional cost, is the opportunity cost equal to what a firm must give up in order to use factors which it neither purchases nor hires. It is the opposite of an explicit cost, which is borne directly. In other words, an implicit cost is any cost that results from using an asset instead of renting, selling, or lending it.
Explicit cost	An explicit cost is a direct payment made to others in the course of running a business, such as wage, rent and materials, as opposed to implicit costs, which are those where no actual payment is made. It is possible still to underestimate these costs, however: for example, pension contributions and other 'perks' must be taken into account when considering the cost of labour. Explicit costs are taken into account along with implicit ones when considering economic profit.
Opportunity cost	In microeconomic theory, the opportunity cost of a choice is the value of the best alternative forgone, in a situation in which a choice needs to be made between several mutually exclusive alternatives given limited resources. Assuming the best choice is made, it is the 'cost' incurred by not enjoying the benefit that would be had by taking the second best choice available. The New Oxford American Dictionary defines it as 'the loss of potential gain from other alternatives when one alternative is chosen'.
Cost	In production, research, retail, and accounting, a cost is the value of money that has been used up to produce something, and hence is not available for use anymore. In business, the cost may be one of acquisition, in which case the amount of money expended to acquire it is counted as cost. In this case, money is the input that is gone in order to acquire the thing.
Depreciation	In accountancy, depreciation refers to two aspects of the same concept:•the decrease in value of assets (fair value depreciation), and•the allocation of the cost of assets to periods in which the assets are used (depreciation with the matching principle). The former affects the balance sheet of a business or entity, and the latter affects the net income that they report. Generally the cost is allocated, as depreciation expense, among the periods in which the asset is expected to be used. This expense is recognized by businesses for financial reporting and tax purposes.
Overhead	In business, overhead expense refers to an ongoing expense of operating a business; it is also known as an 'operating expense'. Examples include rent, gas, electricity, and labour burden.

3. Benefits, Costs, and Decisions

Selling	Selling is offering to exchange an item of value for a different item. The original item of value being offered may be either tangible or intangible. The second item, usually money, is most often seen by the seller as being of equal or greater value than that being offered for sale.
Generally accepted accounting principles	Generally accepted accounting principles refer to the standard framework of guidelines for financial accounting used in any given jurisdiction; generally known as accounting standards or standard accounting practice. These include the standards, conventions, and rules that accountants follow in recording and summarizing and in the preparation of financial statements.
Lehman Brothers	Lehman Brothers Holdings Inc. (former NYSE ticker symbol LEH) was a global financial services firm. Before declaring bankruptcy in 2008, Lehman was the fourth-largest investment bank in the US (behind Goldman Sachs, Morgan Stanley, and Merrill Lynch), doing business in investment banking, equity and fixed-income sales and trading (especially U.S. Treasury securities), research, investment management, private equity, and private banking.
Subprime mortgage crisis	The U.S. subprime mortgage crisis was a set of events and conditions that were significant aspects of a financial crisis and subsequent recession that became manifestly visible in 2008. It was characterized by a rise in subprime mortgage delinquencies and foreclosures, and the resulting decline of securities backed by said mortgages. These mortgage-backed securities (MBS) and collateralized debt obligations (CDO) initially offered attractive rates of return due to the higher interest rates on the mortgages; however, the lower credit quality ultimately caused massive defaults. While elements of the crisis first became more visible during 2007, several major financial institutions collapsed in September 2008, with significant disruption in the flow of credit to businesses and consumers and the onset of a severe global recession.

CHAPTER QUIZ: KEY TERMS, PEOPLE, PLACES, CONCEPTS

1. In economics, _____ goods, real _____, or _____ assets are already-produced durable goods or any non-financial asset that is used in production of goods or services.

    _____ goods are not significantly consumed in the production process though they may depreciate. How a _____ good or is maintained or returned to its pre-production state varies with the type of _____ involved.

    a. Cigar Box Method
    b. CAPRI model
    c. Cash crop
    d. Capital

3. Benefits, Costs, and Decisions

2. In economics, _____s, indirect costs or overheads are business expenses that are not dependent on the level of goods or services produced by the business. They tend to be time-related, such as salaries or rents being paid per month, and are often referred to as overhead costs. This is in contrast to variable costs, which are volume-related (and are paid per quantity produced).

   a. Business mileage reimbursement rate
   b. Fixed cost
   c. Cost accounting
   d. Cost curve

3. In economics, a _____ is a graph of the costs of production as a function of total quantity produced. In a free market economy, productively efficient firms use these curves to find the optimal point of production (minimizing cost), and profit maximizing firms can use them to decide output quantities to achieve those aims. There are various types of _____s, all related to each other, including total and average _____s, and marginal ('for each additional unit') _____s, which are equal to the differential of the total _____s.

   a. Cost curve
   b. Budget constraint
   c. Contract curve
   d. Preference-rank translation

4. In economics, _____ or unit cost is equal to total cost divided by the number of goods produced . It is also equal to the sum of average variable costs (total variable costs divided by Q) plus average fixed costs (total fixed costs divided by Q). _____s may be dependent on the time period considered (increasing production may be expensive or impossible in the short term, for example).

   a. Cost
   b. Average cost
   c. Federal Reserve
   d. Fuel protests in the United Kingdom

5. _____s are fixed, one-time expenses incurred on the purchase of land, buildings, construction, and equipment used in the production of goods or in the rendering of services. Put simply, it is the total cost needed to bring a project to a commercially operable status. Whether a particular cost is capital or not depend on many factors such as accounting, tax laws, and materiality.

   a. Base period
   b. Benefit incidence
   c. Blanket order
   d. Capital cost

1. d
2. b
3. a
4. b
5. d

You can take the complete Chapter Practice Test

for 3. Benefits, Costs, and Decisions
on all key terms, persons, places, and concepts.

Online 99 Cents

http://www.JustTheFacts101.com

Use www.JustTheFacts101.com for all your study needs

including Facts101's online interactive problem solving labs in

chemistry, statistics, mathematics, and more.

4. Extent Decisions

CHAPTER OUTLINE: KEY TERMS, PEOPLE, PLACES, CONCEPTS

	Subprime mortgage crisis
	Average cost
	Cost curve
	Marginal cost
	Average
	Customer acquisition cost
	Opportunity cost

CHAPTER HIGHLIGHTS & NOTES: KEY TERMS, PEOPLE, PLACES, CONCEPTS

Subprime mortgage crisis	The U.S. subprime mortgage crisis was a set of events and conditions that were significant aspects of a financial crisis and subsequent recession that became manifestly visible in 2008. It was characterized by a rise in subprime mortgage delinquencies and foreclosures, and the resulting decline of securities backed by said mortgages. These mortgage-backed securities (MBS) and collateralized debt obligations (CDO) initially offered attractive rates of return due to the higher interest rates on the mortgages; however, the lower credit quality ultimately caused massive defaults. While elements of the crisis first became more visible during 2007, several major financial institutions collapsed in September 2008, with significant disruption in the flow of credit to businesses and consumers and the onset of a severe global recession.
Average cost	In economics, average cost or unit cost is equal to total cost divided by the number of goods produced . It is also equal to the sum of average variable costs (total variable costs divided by Q) plus average fixed costs (total fixed costs divided by Q). Average costs may be dependent on the time period considered (increasing production may be expensive or impossible in the short term, for example).
Cost curve	In economics, a cost curve is a graph of the costs of production as a function of total quantity produced. In a free market economy, productively efficient firms use these curves to find the optimal point of production (minimizing cost), and profit maximizing firms can use them to decide output quantities to achieve those aims.

4. Extent Decisions

Marginal cost	In economics and finance, marginal cost is the change in the total cost that arises when the quantity produced has an increment by unit. That is, it is the cost of producing one more unit of a good. In general terms, marginal cost at each level of production includes any additional costs required to produce the next unit.
Average	In colloquial language average usually refers to the sum of a list of numbers divided by the size of the list, in other words the arithmetic mean. However, the word 'average' can be used to refer to the median, the mode, or some other central or typical value. In statistics, these are all known as measures of central tendency.
Customer acquisition cost	Customer Acquisition Cost is the cost associated in convincing a customer to buy a product/service. This cost is incurred by the organization to convince a potential customer. This cost is inclusive of the product cost as well as the cost involved in research, marketing, and accessibility costs.
Opportunity cost	In microeconomic theory, the opportunity cost of a choice is the value of the best alternative forgone, in a situation in which a choice needs to be made between several mutually exclusive alternatives given limited resources. Assuming the best choice is made, it is the 'cost' incurred by not enjoying the benefit that would be had by taking the second best choice available. The New Oxford American Dictionary defines it as 'the loss of potential gain from other alternatives when one alternative is chosen'.

1. The U.S. _____ was a set of events and conditions that were significant aspects of a financial crisis and subsequent recession that became manifestly visible in 2008. It was characterized by a rise in subprime mortgage delinquencies and foreclosures, and the resulting decline of securities backed by said mortgages. These mortgage-backed securities (MBS) and collateralized debt obligations (CDO) initially offered attractive rates of return due to the higher interest rates on the mortgages; however, the lower credit quality ultimately caused massive defaults. While elements of the crisis first became more visible during 2007, several major financial institutions collapsed in September 2008, with significant disruption in the flow of credit to businesses and consumers and the onset of a severe global recession.

   a. Subprime mortgage crisis
   b. Bank failure
   c. Local currency
   d. Demand for money

2. . In economics, _____ or unit cost is equal to total cost divided by the number of goods produced . It is also equal to the sum of average variable costs (total variable costs divided by Q) plus average fixed costs (total fixed costs divided by Q).

_____s may be dependent on the time period considered (increasing production may be expensive or impossible in the short term, for example).

a. Average cost
b. cost reduction
c. Federal Reserve
d. Fuel protests in the United Kingdom

3. In economics and finance, _____ is the change in the total cost that arises when the quantity produced has an increment by unit. That is, it is the cost of producing one more unit of a good. In general terms, _____ at each level of production includes any additional costs required to produce the next unit.

a. Benefit principle
b. Marginal cost
c. Club good
d. Conjectural variation

4. In microeconomic theory, the _____ of a choice is the value of the best alternative forgone, in a situation in which a choice needs to be made between several mutually exclusive alternatives given limited resources. Assuming the best choice is made, it is the 'cost' incurred by not enjoying the benefit that would be had by taking the second best choice available. The New Oxford American Dictionary defines it as 'the loss of potential gain from other alternatives when one alternative is chosen'.

a. Opportunity cost
b. Bliss point
c. Club good
d. Conjectural variation

5. In economics, a _____ is a graph of the costs of production as a function of total quantity produced. In a free market economy, productively efficient firms use these curves to find the optimal point of production (minimizing cost), and profit maximizing firms can use them to decide output quantities to achieve those aims. There are various types of _____s, all related to each other, including total and average _____s, and marginal ('for each additional unit') _____s, which are equal to the differential of the total _____s.

a. Beveridge curve
b. Budget constraint
c. Contract curve
d. Cost curve

1. a

2. a

3. b

4. a

5. d

You can take the complete Chapter Practice Test

for 4. Extent Decisions
on all key terms, persons, places, and concepts.

Online 99 Cents

http://www.JustTheFacts101.com

Use www.JustTheFacts101.com for all your study needs

including Facts101's online interactive problem solving labs in

chemistry, statistics, mathematics, and more.

5. Investment Decisions: Look Ahead and Reason Back

	Discounting
	Weighted average cost of capital
	Average cost
	Cost
	Future value
	Internet
	Present value
	Adverse selection
	Value
	Economic profit
	Marginal cost
	Cost curve
	Fixed cost
	Outsourcing
	Variable
	Variable cost
	Sunk costs

Discounting	Discounting is a financial mechanism in which a debtor obtains the right to delay payments to a creditor, for a defined period of time, in exchange for a charge or fee. Essentially, the party that owes money in the present purchases the right to delay the payment until some future date. The discount, or charge, is the difference between the original amount owed in the present and the amount that has to be paid in the future to settle the debt.
Weighted average cost of capital	The weighted average cost of capital is the rate that a company is expected to pay on average to all its security holders to finance its assets. The WACC is the minimum return that a company must earn on an existing asset base to satisfy its creditors, owners, and other providers of capital, or they will invest elsewhere. Companies raise money from a number of sources: common equity, preferred stock, straight debt, convertible debt, exchangeable debt, warrants, options, pension liabilities, executive stock options, governmental subsidies, and so on.
Average cost	In economics, average cost or unit cost is equal to total cost divided by the number of goods produced . It is also equal to the sum of average variable costs (total variable costs divided by Q) plus average fixed costs (total fixed costs divided by Q). Average costs may be dependent on the time period considered (increasing production may be expensive or impossible in the short term, for example).
Cost	In production, research, retail, and accounting, a cost is the value of money that has been used up to produce something, and hence is not available for use anymore. In business, the cost may be one of acquisition, in which case the amount of money expended to acquire it is counted as cost. In this case, money is the input that is gone in order to acquire the thing.
Future value	Future value is the value of an asset at a specific date. It measures the nominal future sum of money that a given sum of money is 'worth' at a specified time in the future assuming a certain interest rate, or more generally, rate of return; it is the present value multiplied by the accumulation function. The value does not include corrections for inflation or other factors that affect the true value of money in the future.
Internet	The Internet is a global system of interconnected computer networks that use the standard Internet protocol suite to link several billion devices worldwide. It is a network of networks that consists of millions of private, public, academic, business, and government networks, of local to global scope, that are linked by a broad array of electronic, wireless, and optical networking technologies. The Internet carries an extensive range of information resources and services, such as the inter-linked hypertext documents and applications of the World Wide Web (WWW), the infrastructure to support email, and peer-to-peer networks for file sharing and telephony.
Present value	Present value, also known as present discounted value, is a future amount of money that has been discounted to reflect its current value, as if it existed today.

	The present value is always less than or equal to the future value because money has interest-earning potential, a characteristic referred to as the time value of money. Time value can be described with the simplified phrase, "A dollar today is worth more than a dollar tomorrow".
Adverse selection	Adverse selection, anti-selection, or negative selection is a term used in economics, insurance, risk management, and statistics. It refers to a market process in which undesired results occur when buyers and sellers have asymmetric information (access to different information); the 'bad' products or services are more likely to be selected. For example, a bank that sets one price for all of its checking account customers runs the risk of being adversely selected against by its low-balance, high-activity (and hence least profitable) customers.
Value	Economic value is a measure of the benefit that an economic actor can gain from either a good or service. It is generally measured relative to units of currency, and the interpretation is therefore 'what is the maximum amount of money a specific actor is willing and able to pay for the good or service'? Note that economic value is not the same as market price. If a consumer is willing to buy a good, it implies that the customer places a higher value on the good than the market price.
Economic profit	In neoclassical microeconomic theory, the term profit has two related but distinct meanings. Economic profit is similar to accounting profit but smaller because it reflects the total opportunity costs (both explicit and implicit) of a venture to an investor. Normal profit refers to a situation in which the economic profit is zero.
Marginal cost	In economics and finance, marginal cost is the change in the total cost that arises when the quantity produced has an increment by unit. That is, it is the cost of producing one more unit of a good. In general terms, marginal cost at each level of production includes any additional costs required to produce the next unit.
Cost curve	In economics, a cost curve is a graph of the costs of production as a function of total quantity produced. In a free market economy, productively efficient firms use these curves to find the optimal point of production (minimizing cost), and profit maximizing firms can use them to decide output quantities to achieve those aims. There are various types of cost curves, all related to each other, including total and average cost curves, and marginal ('for each additional unit') cost curves, which are equal to the differential of the total cost curves.
Fixed cost	In economics, fixed costs, indirect costs or overheads are business expenses that are not dependent on the level of goods or services produced by the business. They tend to be time-related, such as salaries or rents being paid per month, and are often referred to as overhead costs. This is in contrast to variable costs, which are volume-related (and are paid per quantity produced).

Outsourcing	In business, outsourcing is the contracting out of a business process to a third-party. The term 'outsourcing' became popular in the United States near the turn of the 21st century. Outsourcing sometimes involves transferring employees and assets from one firm to another, but not always.
Variable	In elementary mathematics, a variable is an alphabetic character representing a number which is either arbitrary or not fully specified or unknown. Making algebraic computations with variables as if they were explicit numbers allows one to solve a range of problems in a single computation. A typical example is the quadratic formula, which allows to solve every quadratic equation by simply substituting the numeric values of the coefficients of the given equation to the variables that represent them.
Variable cost	Variable costs are costs that change in proportion to the good or service that a business produces. Variable costs are also the sum of marginal costs over all units produced. They can also be considered normal costs.
Sunk costs	In economics and business decision-making, a sunk cost is a retrospective cost that has already been incurred and cannot be recovered. Sunk costs are sometimes contrasted with prospective costs, which are future costs that may be incurred or changed if an action is taken. Both retrospective and prospective costs may be either fixed (continuous for as long as the business is in operation and unaffected by output volume) or variable (dependent on volume) costs.

CHAPTER QUIZ: KEY TERMS, PEOPLE, PLACES, CONCEPTS

1. _____s are costs that change in proportion to the good or service that a business produces. _____s are also the sum of marginal costs over all units produced. They can also be considered normal costs.

   a. Business mileage reimbursement rate
   b. Cost
   c. Cost accounting
   d. Variable cost

2. . In economics and finance, _____ is the change in the total cost that arises when the quantity produced has an increment by unit. That is, it is the cost of producing one more unit of a good. In general terms, _____ at each level of production includes any additional costs required to produce the next unit.

   a. Benefit principle
   b. Bliss point
   c. Club good

3. The _____ is a global system of interconnected computer networks that use the standard _____ protocol suite to link several billion devices worldwide. It is a network of networks that consists of millions of private, public, academic, business, and government networks, of local to global scope, that are linked by a broad array of electronic, wireless, and optical networking technologies. The _____ carries an extensive range of information resources and services, such as the inter-linked hypertext documents and applications of the World Wide Web (WWW), the infrastructure to support email, and peer-to-peer networks for file sharing and telephony.

    a. Brain drain
    b. Cultural homogenization
    c. Democratization of technology
    d. Internet

4. _____ is the value of an asset at a specific date. It measures the nominal future sum of money that a given sum of money is 'worth' at a specified time in the future assuming a certain interest rate, or more generally, rate of return; it is the present value multiplied by the accumulation function. The value does not include corrections for inflation or other factors that affect the true value of money in the future.

    a. Future value
    b. Cash accumulation equation
    c. Cointegration
    d. Consumer math

5. The _____ is the rate that a company is expected to pay on average to all its security holders to finance its assets.

The WACC is the minimum return that a company must earn on an existing asset base to satisfy its creditors, owners, and other providers of capital, or they will invest elsewhere. Companies raise money from a number of sources: common equity, preferred stock, straight debt, convertible debt, exchangeable debt, warrants, options, pension liabilities, executive stock options, governmental subsidies, and so on.

    a. Bond equivalent yield
    b. Weighted average cost of capital
    c. Cointegration
    d. Consumer math

1. d
2. d
3. d
4. a
5. b

6. Simple Pricing

CHAPTER OUTLINE: KEY TERMS, PEOPLE, PLACES, CONCEPTS

Product

Consumer

Consumer surplus

Simple

Value

Aggregate demand

Cost curve

Marginal cost

Elasticity

Elasticity of demand

Price discrimination

Cost

Cost price

Marginal revenue

Loss leader

Demand

Demand forecasting

Forecasting

Cross-price elasticity of demand

Mattel

Present value

6. Simple Pricing

	Taxes
	Income

Product	In marketing, a product is anything that can be offered to a market that might satisfy a want or need. In retailing, products are called merchandise. In manufacturing, products are bought as raw materials and sold as finished goods.
Consumer	A consumer is a person or group of people, such as a household, who are the final users of products or services. The consumer's use is final in the sense that the product is usually not improved by the use.
Consumer surplus	In mainstream economics, economic surplus (also known as total welfare or Marshallian surplus) refers to two related quantities. Consumer surplus or consumers' surplus is the monetary gain obtained by consumers because they are able to purchase a product for a price that is less than the highest price that they would be willing to pay. Producer surplus or producers' surplus is the amount that producers benefit by selling at a market price that is higher than the least that they would be willing to sell for.
Simple	In contemporary mereology, a simple is any thing that has no proper parts. Sometimes the term 'atom' is used, although in recent years the term 'simple' has become the standard. Simples are to be contrasted with atomless gunk (where something is 'gunky' if it is such that every proper part has a further proper part).
Value	Economic value is a measure of the benefit that an economic actor can gain from either a good or service. It is generally measured relative to units of currency, and the interpretation is therefore 'what is the maximum amount of money a specific actor is willing and able to pay for the good or service'? Note that economic value is not the same as market price. If a consumer is willing to buy a good, it implies that the customer places a higher value on the good than the market price.
Aggregate demand	In economics, aggregate behavior refers to relationships between economic aggregates such as national income, government expenditure and aggregate demand.

For example, the consumption function is a relationship between aggregate demand for consumption and aggregate disposable income.

Models of aggregate behavior may be derived from direct observation of the economy, or from models of individual behavior.

Cost curve	In economics, a cost curve is a graph of the costs of production as a function of total quantity produced. In a free market economy, productively efficient firms use these curves to find the optimal point of production (minimizing cost), and profit maximizing firms can use them to decide output quantities to achieve those aims. There are various types of cost curves, all related to each other, including total and average cost curves, and marginal ('for each additional unit') cost curves, which are equal to the differential of the total cost curves.
Marginal cost	In economics and finance, marginal cost is the change in the total cost that arises when the quantity produced has an increment by unit. That is, it is the cost of producing one more unit of a good. In general terms, marginal cost at each level of production includes any additional costs required to produce the next unit.
Elasticity	In economics, elasticity is the measurement of how responsive an economic variable is to a change in another. For example:•'If I lower the price of my product, how much more will I sell?'•'If I raise the price of one good, how will that affect sales of this other good?'•'If we learn that a resource is becoming scarce, will people scramble to acquire it?' An elastic variable (or elasticity value greater than 1) is one which responds more than proportionally to changes in other variables. In contrast, an inelastic variable (or elasticity value less than 1) is one which changes less than proportionally in response to changes in other variables.
Elasticity of demand	Price elasticity of demand is a measure used in economics to show the responsiveness, or elasticity, of the quantity demanded of a good or service to a change in its price. More precisely, it gives the percentage change in quantity demanded in response to a one percent change in price (ceteris paribus, i.e. holding constant all the other determinants of demand, such as income). Price elasticities are almost always negative, although analysts tend to ignore the sign even though this can lead to ambiguity.
Price discrimination	Price discrimination or price differentiation is a pricing strategy where identical or largely similar goods or services are transacted at different prices by the same provider in different markets or territories. Price differentiation is distinguished from product differentiation by the more substantial difference in production cost for the differently priced products involved in the latter strategy. Price differentiation essentially relies on the variation in the customers' willingness to pay.

6. Simple Pricing

Cost	In production, research, retail, and accounting, a cost is the value of money that has been used up to produce something, and hence is not available for use anymore. In business, the cost may be one of acquisition, in which case the amount of money expended to acquire it is counted as cost. In this case, money is the input that is gone in order to acquire the thing.
Cost price	In retail systems, the cost price represents the specific value that represents unit price purchased. This value is used as a key factor in determining profitability, and in some stock market theories it is used in establishing the value of stock holding.
Marginal revenue	In microeconomics, marginal revenue is the additional revenue that will be generated by increasing product sales by 1 unit. It can also be described as the unit revenue the last item sold has generated for the firm. In a perfectly competitive market, the additional revenue generated by selling an additional unit of a good is equal to the price the firm is able to charge the buyer of the good.
Loss leader	A loss leader is a pricing strategy where a product is sold at a price below its market cost to stimulate other sales of more profitable goods or services. With this sales promotion--marketing strategy, a 'leader' is used as a related term and can mean any popular article, i.e., one sold at a normal price.
Demand	In economics, demand for a good or service is an entire listing of the quantity of the good or service that a market would choose to buy, for every possible market price of the good or service. (Note: This distinguishes 'demand' from 'quantity demanded', where demand is a listing or graphing of quantity demanded at each possible price. In contrast to demand, quantity demanded is the exact quantity demanded at a certain price.
Demand forecasting	Demand forecasting is the activity of estimating the quantity of a product or service that consumers will purchase. Demand forecasting involves techniques including both informal methods, such as educated guesses, and quantitative methods, such as the use of historical sales data or current data from test markets. Demand forecasting may be used in making pricing decisions, in assessing future capacity requirements, or in making decisions on whether to enter a new market.
Forecasting	Forecasting is the process of making statements about events whose actual outcomes have not yet been observed. A commonplace example might be estimation of some variable of interest at some specified future date. Prediction is a similar, but more general term.
Cross-price elasticity of demand	In economics, the cross elasticity of demand or cross-price elasticity of demand measures the responsiveness of the demand for a good to a change in the price of another good. It is measured as the percentage change in demand for the first good that occurs in response to a percentage change in price of the second good. For example, if, in response to a 10% increase in the price of fuel, the demand of new cars that are fuel inefficient decreased by 20%, the cross elasticity of demand would be:

6. Simple Pricing

Mattel	Mattel, Inc. is an American toy manufacturing company founded in 1945 with headquarters in El Segundo, California. In 2008, it ranked #413 on the Fortune 500. The products and brands it produces include Fisher-Price, Barbie dolls, Monster High dolls, Hot Wheels and Matchbox toys, Masters of the Universe, American Girl dolls, board games, WWE Toys, and early-1980s video game systems.
Present value	Present value, also known as present discounted value, is a future amount of money that has been discounted to reflect its current value, as if it existed today. The present value is always less than or equal to the future value because money has interest-earning potential, a characteristic referred to as the time value of money. Time value can be described with the simplified phrase, "A dollar today is worth more than a dollar tomorrow".
Taxes	A tax is a financial charge or other levy imposed upon a taxpayer (an individual or legal entity) by a state or the functional equivalent of a state such that failure to pay is punishable by law. Taxes are also imposed by many administrative divisions. Taxes consist of direct or indirect taxes and may be paid in money or as its labour equivalent.
Income	Income is the consumption and savings opportunity gained by an entity within a specified timeframe, which is generally expressed in monetary terms. However, for households and individuals, 'income is the sum of all the wages, salaries, profits, interests payments, rents and other forms of earnings received... in a given period of time.' In the field of public economics, the term may refer to the accumulation of both monetary and non-monetary consumption ability, with the former (monetary) being used as a proxy for total income.

CHAPTER QUIZ: KEY TERMS, PEOPLE, PLACES, CONCEPTS

---

1. A _____ is a person or group of people, such as a household, who are the final users of products or services. The _____'s use is final in the sense that the product is usually not improved by the use.

   a. Bliss point
   b. Consumer
   c. Budget set
   d. Complementary good

2. . In economics, aggregate behavior refers to relationships between economic aggregates such as national income, government expenditure and _____. For example, the consumption function is a relationship between _____ for consumption and aggregate disposable income.

Models of aggregate behavior may be derived from direct observation of the economy, or from models of individual behavior.

a. Bad bank
b. Aggregate demand
c. Jewish Social Democratic Party
d. Communist Bund

3. In contemporary mereology, a _____ is any thing that has no proper parts. Sometimes the term 'atom' is used, although in recent years the term '_____' has become the standard.

_____s are to be contrasted with atomless gunk (where something is 'gunky' if it is such that every proper part has a further proper part).

a. Bayesian probability
b. Berlin Circle
c. Simple
d. Biological determinism

4. _____ or price differentiation is a pricing strategy where identical or largely similar goods or services are transacted at different prices by the same provider in different markets or territories. Price differentiation is distinguished from product differentiation by the more substantial difference in production cost for the differently priced products involved in the latter strategy. Price differentiation essentially relies on the variation in the customers' willingness to pay.

a. Benefit principle
b. Bliss point
c. Club good
d. Price discrimination

5. Economic _____ is a measure of the benefit that an economic actor can gain from either a good or service. It is generally measured relative to units of currency, and the interpretation is therefore 'what is the maximum amount of money a specific actor is willing and able to pay for the good or service'?

Note that economic _____ is not the same as market price. If a consumer is willing to buy a good, it implies that the customer places a higher _____ on the good than the market price.

a. Benefit principle
b. Bliss point
c. Value
d. Conjectural variation

1. b
2. b
3. c
4. d
5. c

You can take the complete Chapter Practice Test

for 6. Simple Pricing
on all key terms, persons, places, and concepts.

Online 99 Cents

http://www.JustTheFacts101.com

Use www.JustTheFacts101.com for all your study needs

including Facts101's online interactive problem solving labs in

chemistry, statistics, mathematics, and more.

7. Economies of Scale and Scope

CHAPTER OUTLINE: KEY TERMS, PEOPLE, PLACES, CONCEPTS

Economies of scale

Economies of scope

Cost curve

Marginal cost

Average cost

Learning curve

Returns

Manufacturing cost

Airbus

Antitrust law

Antitrust

Efficiency

Economics

7. Economies of Scale and Scope

Economies of scale	In microeconomics, economies of scale are the cost advantages that enterprises obtain due to size, output, or scale of operation, with cost per unit of output generally decreasing with increasing scale as fixed costs are spread out over more units of output.
	Often operational efficiency is also greater with increasing scale, leading to lower variable cost as well.
	Economies of scale apply to a variety of organizational and business situations and at various levels, such as a business or manufacturing unit, plant or an entire enterprise.
Economies of scope	Economies of scope are conceptually similar to economies of scale. Whereas economies of scale for a firm primarily refers to reductions in the average cost (cost per unit) associated with increasing the scale of production for a single product type, economies of scope refers to lowering the average cost for a firm in producing two or more products. The term and the concept's development are attributed to Panzar and Willig (1977, 1981).
Cost curve	In economics, a cost curve is a graph of the costs of production as a function of total quantity produced. In a free market economy, productively efficient firms use these curves to find the optimal point of production (minimizing cost), and profit maximizing firms can use them to decide output quantities to achieve those aims. There are various types of cost curves, all related to each other, including total and average cost curves, and marginal ('for each additional unit') cost curves, which are equal to the differential of the total cost curves.
Marginal cost	In economics and finance, marginal cost is the change in the total cost that arises when the quantity produced has an increment by unit. That is, it is the cost of producing one more unit of a good. In general terms, marginal cost at each level of production includes any additional costs required to produce the next unit.
Average cost	In economics, average cost or unit cost is equal to total cost divided by the number of goods produced . It is also equal to the sum of average variable costs (total variable costs divided by Q) plus average fixed costs (total fixed costs divided by Q). Average costs may be dependent on the time period considered (increasing production may be expensive or impossible in the short term, for example).
Learning curve	A learning curve is a graphical representation of the increase of learning with experience (horizontal axis).
	Although the curve for a single subject may be erratic (Fig 1), when a large number of trials are averaged, a smooth curve results, which can be described with a mathematical function (Fig 2). Depending on the metric used for learning (or proficiency) the curve can either rise or fall with experience (Fig 3).

7. Economies of Scale and Scope

Returns	Returns, in economics and political economy, are the distributions or payments awarded to the various suppliers of the factors of production.
Manufacturing cost	Manufacturing cost is the sum of costs of all resources consumed in the process of making a product. The manufacturing cost is classified into three categories: direct materials cost, direct labor cost and manufacturing overhead.
Airbus	Airbus SAS is an aircraft manufacturing division of Airbus Group (formerly European Aeronautic Defence and Space Company). Based in Blagnac, France, a suburb of Toulouse, with production and manufacturing facilities mainly in France, Germany, Spain and the United Kingdom, the company produced 626 airliners in 2013. Airbus began as a consortium of aerospace manufacturers, Airbus Industrie.
Antitrust law	Competition law is law that promotes or seeks to maintain market competition by regulating anti-competitive conduct by companies. Competition law is implemented through Public and Private Enforcement Competition law is known as antitrust law in the United States and anti-monopoly law in China and Russia. In previous years it has been known as trade practices law in the United Kingdom and Australia.
Antitrust	Competition law is law that promotes or seeks to maintain market competition by regulating anti-competitive conduct by companies. Competition law is known as antitrust law in the United States and anti-monopoly law in China and Russia. In previous years it has been known as trade practices law in the United Kingdom and Australia.
Efficiency	The relative efficiency of two procedures is the ratio of their efficiencies, although often this term is used where the comparison is made between a given procedure and a notional 'best possible' procedure. The efficiencies and the relative efficiency of two procedures theoretically depend on the sample size available for the given procedure, but it is often possible to use the asymptotic relative efficiency as the principal comparison measure. Efficiencies are often defined using the variance or mean square error as the measure of desirability.
Economics	Economics is the social science that studies the behavior of individuals, groups, and organizations, when they manage or use scarce resources, which have alternative uses, to achieve desired ends.

7. Economies of Scale and Scope

Agents are assumed to act rationally, have multiple desirable ends in sight, limited resources to obtain these ends, a set of stable preferences, a definite overall guiding objective, and the capability of making a choice. There exists an economic problem, subject to study by economic science, when a decision (choice) has to be made by one or more resource-controlling players to attain the best possible outcome under bounded rational conditions.

1. Competition law is law that promotes or seeks to maintain market competition by regulating anti-competitive conduct by companies.

   Competition law is known as _____ law in the United States and anti-monopoly law in China and Russia. In previous years it has been known as trade practices law in the United Kingdom and Australia.

   a. Enterprise Act 2002
   b. Essential facilities doctrine
   c. Antitrust
   d. European Union merger law

2. In economics, a _____ is a graph of the costs of production as a function of total quantity produced. In a free market economy, productively efficient firms use these curves to find the optimal point of production (minimizing cost), and profit maximizing firms can use them to decide output quantities to achieve those aims. There are various types of _____s, all related to each other, including total and average _____s, and marginal ('for each additional unit') _____s, which are equal to the differential of the total _____s.

   a. Beveridge curve
   b. Budget constraint
   c. Cost curve
   d. Preference-rank translation

3. . In microeconomics, _____ are the cost advantages that enterprises obtain due to size, output, or scale of operation, with cost per unit of output generally decreasing with increasing scale as fixed costs are spread out over more units of output.

   Often operational efficiency is also greater with increasing scale, leading to lower variable cost as well.

   _____ apply to a variety of organizational and business situations and at various levels, such as a business or manufacturing unit, plant or an entire enterprise.

    a. Economies of scale
    b. Constant elasticity of substitution
    c. Constant elasticity of transformation
    d. Cost-of-production theory of value

4.   _____ is the sum of costs of all resources consumed in the process of making a product. The _____ is classified into three categories: direct materials cost, direct labor cost and manufacturing overhead.

    a. Business mileage reimbursement rate
    b. Cost
    c. Cost accounting
    d. Manufacturing cost

5.   _____ are conceptually similar to economies of scale. Whereas economies of scale for a firm primarily refers to reductions in the average cost (cost per unit) associated with increasing the scale of production for a single product type, _____ refers to lowering the average cost for a firm in producing two or more products. The term and the concept's development are attributed to Panzar and Willig (1977, 1981).

    a. Benefit principle
    b. Bliss point
    c. Club good
    d. Economies of scope

1. c
2. c
3. a
4. d
5. d

You can take the complete Chapter Practice Test

for 7. Economies of Scale and Scope
on all key terms, persons, places, and concepts.

Online 99 Cents

http://www.JustTheFacts101.com

Use www.JustTheFacts101.com for all your study needs

including Facts101's online interactive problem solving labs in

chemistry, statistics, mathematics, and more.

8. Understanding Markets and Industry Changes

CHAPTER OUTLINE: KEY TERMS, PEOPLE, PLACES, CONCEPTS

_____ | Monopoly

_____ | Industrial organization

_____ | Perfect competition

_____ | Demand

_____ | Profit

_____ | Supply

_____ | Excess supply

_____ | Market equilibrium

_____ | Purchasing power

_____ | Freddie Mac

_____ | Lehman Brothers

_____ | Federal Reserve

_____ | Google

_____ | Present value

_____ | Stock market

_____ | Stock market index

_____ | Market maker

_____ | Competition

_____ | Market

Monopoly	A monopoly (from Greek monos μ???? + polein p??e?? (to sell)) exists when a specific person or enterprise is the only supplier of a particular commodity (this contrasts with a monopsony which relates to a single entity's control of a market to purchase a good or service, and with oligopoly which consists of a few entities dominating an industry). Monopolies are thus characterized by a lack of economic competition to produce the good or service and a lack of viable substitute goods. The verb 'monopolize' refers to the process by which a company gains the ability to raise prices or exclude competitors.
Industrial organization	In economics, industrial organization is a field that builds on the theory of the firm by examining the structure of firms and markets. Industrial organization adds real-world complications to the perfectly competitive model, complications such as transaction costs, limited information, and barriers to entry of new firms that may be associated with imperfect competition. It analyzes determinants of firm and market organization and behavior as between competition and monopoly, including from government actions.
Perfect competition	In economic theory, perfect competition describes markets such that no participants are large enough to have the market power to set the price of a homogeneous product. Because the conditions for perfect competition are strict, there are few if any perfectly competitive markets. Still, buyers and sellers in some auction-type markets, say for commodities or some financial assets, may approximate the concept.
Demand	In economics, demand for a good or service is an entire listing of the quantity of the good or service that a market would choose to buy, for every possible market price of the good or service. (Note: This distinguishes 'demand' from 'quantity demanded', where demand is a listing or graphing of quantity demanded at each possible price. In contrast to demand, quantity demanded is the exact quantity demanded at a certain price.
Profit	In neoclassical microeconomic theory, the term profit has two related but distinct meanings. Economic profit is similar to accounting profit but smaller because it reflects the total opportunity costs (both explicit and implicit) of a venture to an investor. Normal profit refers to a situation in which the economic profit is zero.
Supply	In economics, supply refers to the amount of a product that producers and firms are willing to sell at a given price all other factors being held constant. Usually, supply is plotted as a supply curve showing the relationship of price to the amount of product businesses are willing to sell.
Excess supply	For the opposite, see excess demand.
	In economics, excess supply is a situation in which the quantity of a good or service supplied is more than the quantity demanded, and the price is above the equilibrium level.

8. Understanding Markets and Industry Changes

Market equilibrium	In economics, economic equilibrium is a state where economic forces such as supply and demand are balanced and in the absence of external influences the values of economic variables will not change. For example, in the standard text-book model of perfect competition, equilibrium occurs at the point at which quantity demanded and quantity supplied are equal. Market equilibrium in this case refers to a condition where a market price is established through competition such that the amount of goods or services sought by buyers is equal to the amount of goods or services produced by sellers.
Purchasing power	Purchasing power is the number of goods or services that can be purchased with a unit of currency. For example, if one had taken one unit of currency to a store in the 1950s, it is probable that it would have been possible to buy a greater number of items than would today, indicating that one would have had a greater purchasing power in the 1950s. Currency can be either a commodity money, like gold or silver, or fiat currency, or free-floating market-valued currency like US dollars.
Freddie Mac	The Federal Home Loan Mortgage Corporation, known as Freddie Mac, is a public government-sponsored enterprise (GSE), headquartered in the Tyson's Corner CDP in unincorporated Fairfax County, Virginia. The FHLMC was created in 1970 to expand the secondary market for mortgages in the US. Along with other GSEs, Freddie Mac buys mortgages on the secondary market, pools them, and sells them as a mortgage-backed security to investors on the open market. This secondary mortgage market increases the supply of money available for mortgage lending and increases the money available for new home purchases.
Lehman Brothers	Lehman Brothers Holdings Inc. (former NYSE ticker symbol LEH) was a global financial services firm. Before declaring bankruptcy in 2008, Lehman was the fourth-largest investment bank in the US (behind Goldman Sachs, Morgan Stanley, and Merrill Lynch), doing business in investment banking, equity and fixed-income sales and trading (especially U.S. Treasury securities), research, investment management, private equity, and private banking.
Federal Reserve	The Federal Reserve System (also known as the Federal Reserve, and informally as the Fed) is the central banking system of the United States. It was created on December 23, 1913, with the enactment of the Federal Reserve Act, largely in response to a series of financial panics, particularly a severe panic in 1907. Over time, the roles and responsibilities of the Federal Reserve System have expanded, and its structure has evolved. Events such as the Great Depression were major factors leading to changes in the system.
Google	Google is an American multinational corporation specializing in Internet-related services and products. These include search, cloud computing, software, and online advertising technologies. Most of its profits are derived from AdWords.

Present value	Present value, also known as present discounted value, is a future amount of money that has been discounted to reflect its current value, as if it existed today. The present value is always less than or equal to the future value because money has interest-earning potential, a characteristic referred to as the time value of money. Time value can be described with the simplified phrase, "A dollar today is worth more than a dollar tomorrow".
Stock market	A stock market or equity market is the aggregation of buyers and sellers of stocks (shares); these are securities listed on a stock exchange as well as those only traded privately.
Stock market index	A stock index or stock market index is a method of measuring the value of a section of the stock market. It is computed from the prices of selected stocks (typically a weighted average). It is a tool used by investors and financial managers to describe the market, and to compare the return on specific investments.
Market maker	A market maker or liquidity provider is a company, or an individual, that quotes both a buy and a sell price in a financial instrument or commodity held in inventory, hoping to make a profit on the bid-offer spread, or turn.
Competition	In economics, competition is the rivalry among sellers trying to achieve such goals as increasing profits, market share, and sales volume by varying the elements of the marketing mix: price, product, distribution, and promotion. Merriam-Webster defines competition in business as 'the effort of two or more parties acting independently to secure the business of a third party by offering the most favorable terms.' It was described by Adam Smith in The Wealth of Nations (1776) and later economists as allocating productive resources to their most highly-valued uses and encouraging efficiency. Smith and other classical economists before Cournot were referring to price and non-price rivalry among producers to sell their goods on best terms by bidding of buyers, not necessarily to a large number of sellers nor to a market in final equilibrium.
Market	A market is one of the many varieties of systems, institutions, procedures, social relations and infrastructures whereby parties engage in exchange. While parties may exchange goods and services by barter, most markets rely on sellers offering their goods or services (including labor) in exchange for money from buyers. It can be said that a market is the process by which the prices of goods and services are established.

8. Understanding Markets and Industry Changes

1. The Federal Home Loan Mortgage Corporation, known as _____, is a public government-sponsored enterprise (GSE), headquartered in the Tyson's Corner CDP in unincorporated Fairfax County, Virginia.

   The FHLMC was created in 1970 to expand the secondary market for mortgages in the US. Along with other GSEs, _____ buys mortgages on the secondary market, pools them, and sells them as a mortgage-backed security to investors on the open market. This secondary mortgage market increases the supply of money available for mortgage lending and increases the money available for new home purchases.

   a. Brevard Family of Housing
   b. Center for Housing Policy
   c. Champlain Housing Trust
   d. Freddie Mac

2. In economic theory, _____ describes markets such that no participants are large enough to have the market power to set the price of a homogeneous product. Because the conditions for _____ are strict, there are few if any perfectly competitive markets. Still, buyers and sellers in some auction-type markets, say for commodities or some financial assets, may approximate the concept.

   a. Perfect competition
   b. Free entry
   c. Hold-up problem
   d. Limit price

3. A _____ (from Greek monos μ???? + polein p??e?? (to sell)) exists when a specific person or enterprise is the only supplier of a particular commodity (this contrasts with a monopsony which relates to a single entity's control of a market to purchase a good or service, and with oligopoly which consists of a few entities dominating an industry). _____(ies) are thus characterized by a lack of economic competition to produce the good or service and a lack of viable substitute goods. The verb 'monopolize' refers to the process by which a company gains the ability to raise prices or exclude competitors.

   a. Contract farming
   b. Convertible husbandry
   c. Monopoly
   d. Community-supported agriculture

4. In neoclassical microeconomic theory, the term _____ has two related but distinct meanings. Economic _____ is similar to accounting _____ but smaller because it reflects the total opportunity costs (both explicit and implicit) of a venture to an investor. Normal _____ refers to a situation in which the economic _____ is zero.

   a. Benefit principle
   b. Profit
   c. Club good
   d. Conjectural variation

5. _____ is an American multinational corporation specializing in Internet-related services and products. These include search, cloud computing, software, and online advertising technologies. Most of its profits are derived from AdWords.

   a. Backlink
   b. Blackstartup
   c. Google
   d. Chief web officer

1. d
2. a
3. c
4. b
5. c

You can take the complete Chapter Practice Test

for 8. Understanding Markets and Industry Changes
on all key terms, persons, places, and concepts.

Online 99 Cents

http://www.JustTheFacts101.com

Use www.JustTheFacts101.com for all your study needs

including Facts101's online interactive problem solving labs in

chemistry, statistics, mathematics, and more.

CHAPTER OUTLINE: KEY TERMS, PEOPLE, PLACES, CONCEPTS

	Subprime mortgage crisis
	Short run
	Demand shock
	Mean reversion
	Supply shock
	Risk premium
	Stock market
	Stock market index
	Equity risk
	Competition
	Elasticity
	Elasticity of demand
	Monopoly
	Samsung

9. Relationships Between Industries: The Forces Moving Us Toward Long-Run ...

CHAPTER HIGHLIGHTS & NOTES: KEY TERMS, PEOPLE, PLACES, CONCEPTS

Subprime mortgage crisis	The U.S. subprime mortgage crisis was a set of events and conditions that were significant aspects of a financial crisis and subsequent recession that became manifestly visible in 2008. It was characterized by a rise in subprime mortgage delinquencies and foreclosures, and the resulting decline of securities backed by said mortgages. These mortgage-backed securities (MBS) and collateralized debt obligations (CDO) initially offered attractive rates of return due to the higher interest rates on the mortgages; however, the lower credit quality ultimately caused massive defaults. While elements of the crisis first became more visible during 2007, several major financial institutions collapsed in September 2008, with significant disruption in the flow of credit to businesses and consumers and the onset of a severe global recession.
Short run	In microeconomics, the long run is the conceptual time period in which there are no fixed factors of production as to changing the output level by changing the capital stock or by entering or leaving an industry. The long run contrasts with the short run, in which some factors are variable and others are fixed, constraining entry or exit from an industry. In macroeconomics, the long run is the period when the general price level, contractual wage rates, and expectations adjust fully to the state of the economy, in contrast to the short run when these variables may not fully adjust.
Demand shock	In economics, a demand shock is a sudden event that increases or decreases demand for goods or services temporarily.
Mean reversion	Mean reversion is a mathematical concept sometimes used for stock investing, but it can be applied to other assets. In general terms, the essence of the concept is the assumption that both a stock's high and low prices are temporary and that a stock's price will tend to move to the average price over time. Using mean reversion in stock price analysis involves both identifying the trading range for a stock and computing the average price using analytical techniques taking into account considerations such as earnings, etc.
Supply shock	A supply shock is an event that suddenly changes the price of a commodity or service. It may be caused by a sudden increase or decrease in the supply of a particular good. This sudden change affects the equilibrium price.
Risk premium	Risk premium is the minimum amount of money by which the expected return on a risky asset must exceed the known return on a risk-free asset, or the expected return on a less risky asset, in order to induce an individual to hold the risky asset rather than the risk-free asset. (Note that risk premia may be negative). Thus it is the minimum willingness to accept compensation for the risk.
Stock market	A stock market or equity market is the aggregation of buyers and sellers of stocks (shares); these are securities listed on a stock exchange as well as those only traded privately.

9. Relationships Between Industries: The Forces Moving Us Toward Long-Run ...

61

Stock market index	A stock index or stock market index is a method of measuring the value of a section of the stock market. It is computed from the prices of selected stocks (typically a weighted average). It is a tool used by investors and financial managers to describe the market, and to compare the return on specific investments.
Equity risk	Equity risk is 'the financial risk involved in holding equity in a particular investment.' Equity risk often refers to equity in companies through the purchase of stocks, and does not commonly refer to the risk in paying into real estate or building equity in properties.
	The measure of risk used in the equity markets is typically the standard deviation of a security's price over a number of periods. The standard deviation will delineate the normal fluctuations one can expect in that particular security above and below the mean, or average.
Competition	In economics, competition is the rivalry among sellers trying to achieve such goals as increasing profits, market share, and sales volume by varying the elements of the marketing mix: price, product, distribution, and promotion. Merriam-Webster defines competition in business as 'the effort of two or more parties acting independently to secure the business of a third party by offering the most favorable terms.' It was described by Adam Smith in The Wealth of Nations (1776) and later economists as allocating productive resources to their most highly-valued uses and encouraging efficiency. Smith and other classical economists before Cournot were referring to price and non-price rivalry among producers to sell their goods on best terms by bidding of buyers, not necessarily to a large number of sellers nor to a market in final equilibrium.
Elasticity	In economics, elasticity is the measurement of how responsive an economic variable is to a change in another. For example:•'If I lower the price of my product, how much more will I sell?'•'If I raise the price of one good, how will that affect sales of this other good?'•'If we learn that a resource is becoming scarce, will people scramble to acquire it?'
	An elastic variable (or elasticity value greater than 1) is one which responds more than proportionally to changes in other variables. In contrast, an inelastic variable (or elasticity value less than 1) is one which changes less than proportionally in response to changes in other variables.
Elasticity of demand	Price elasticity of demand is a measure used in economics to show the responsiveness, or elasticity, of the quantity demanded of a good or service to a change in its price. More precisely, it gives the percentage change in quantity demanded in response to a one percent change in price (ceteris paribus, i.e. holding constant all the other determinants of demand, such as income).
	Price elasticities are almost always negative, although analysts tend to ignore the sign even though this can lead to ambiguity.

Monopoly	A monopoly (from Greek monos μ???? + polein p??e?? (to sell)) exists when a specific person or enterprise is the only supplier of a particular commodity (this contrasts with a monopsony which relates to a single entity's control of a market to purchase a good or service, and with oligopoly which consists of a few entities dominating an industry). Monopolies are thus characterized by a lack of economic competition to produce the good or service and a lack of viable substitute goods. The verb 'monopolize' refers to the process by which a company gains the ability to raise prices or exclude competitors.
Samsung	Samsung Group is a South Korean multinational conglomerate company headquartered in Samsung Town, Seoul. It comprises numerous subsidiaries and affiliated businesses, most of them united under the Samsung brand, and is the largest South Korean chaebol (business conglomerate). Samsung was founded by Lee Byung-chul in 1938 as a trading company.

1. A _____ (from Greek monos μ???? + polein p??e?? (to sell)) exists when a specific person or enterprise is the only supplier of a particular commodity (this contrasts with a monopsony which relates to a single entity's control of a market to purchase a good or service, and with oligopoly which consists of a few entities dominating an industry). _____(ies) are thus characterized by a lack of economic competition to produce the good or service and a lack of viable substitute goods. The verb 'monopolize' refers to the process by which a company gains the ability to raise prices or exclude competitors.

   a. Contract farming
   b. Monopoly
   c. Corn exchange
   d. Community-supported agriculture

2. A _____ is an event that suddenly changes the price of a commodity or service. It may be caused by a sudden increase or decrease in the supply of a particular good. This sudden change affects the equilibrium price.

   a. Boukaseff scale
   b. Bureau de change
   c. Supply shock
   d. Classical dichotomy

3. . The U.S. _____ was a set of events and conditions that were significant aspects of a financial crisis and subsequent recession that became manifestly visible in 2008. It was characterized by a rise in subprime mortgage delinquencies and foreclosures, and the resulting decline of securities backed by said mortgages.

These mortgage-backed securities (MBS) and collateralized debt obligations (CDO) initially offered attractive rates of return due to the higher interest rates on the mortgages; however, the lower credit quality ultimately caused massive defaults. While elements of the crisis first became more visible during 2007, several major financial institutions collapsed in September 2008, with significant disruption in the flow of credit to businesses and consumers and the onset of a severe global recession.

a. Subprime mortgage crisis

b. Bank failure

c. Local currency

d. Demand for money

4. In microeconomics, the long run is the conceptual time period in which there are no fixed factors of production as to changing the output level by changing the capital stock or by entering or leaving an industry. The long run contrasts with the _____, in which some factors are variable and others are fixed, constraining entry or exit from an industry. In macroeconomics, the long run is the period when the general price level, contractual wage rates, and expectations adjust fully to the state of the economy, in contrast to the _____ when these variables may not fully adjust.

a. Gresham's Law

b. Bank failure

c. Short run

d. Demand for money

5. A _____ or equity market is the aggregation of buyers and sellers of stocks (shares); these are securities listed on a stock exchange as well as those only traded privately.

a. Black capitalism

b. Capitalist peace

c. Stock market

d. Caravan capitalism

1. b

2. c

3. a

4. c

5. c

You can take the complete Chapter Practice Test

for 9. Relationships Between Industries: The Forces Moving Us Toward Long-Run ...
on all key terms, persons, places, and concepts.

Online 99 Cents

http://www.JustTheFacts101.com

Use www.JustTheFacts101.com for all your study needs

including Facts101's online interactive problem solving labs in

chemistry, statistics, mathematics, and more.

10. Strategy: The Quest to Keep Profit from Eroding

	Monopoly
	Starbuck
	Competitive advantage
	Industrial organization
	Resource-based view
	Cost
	Cost curve
	Internet
	Product differentiation
	Adverse selection
	Economies of scale

CHAPTER HIGHLIGHTS & NOTES: KEY TERMS, PEOPLE, PLACES, CONCEPTS

Monopoly	A monopoly (from Greek monos μ???? + polein p??e?? (to sell)) exists when a specific person or enterprise is the only supplier of a particular commodity (this contrasts with a monopsony which relates to a single entity's control of a market to purchase a good or service, and with oligopoly which consists of a few entities dominating an industry). Monopolies are thus characterized by a lack of economic competition to produce the good or service and a lack of viable substitute goods. The verb 'monopolize' refers to the process by which a company gains the ability to raise prices or exclude competitors.
Starbuck	The Starbuck family were a group of whalers based in Nantucket, Massachusetts, United States, from the seventeenth to the nineteenth centuries. Some members of the family gained wider exposure due to their discovery of various islands in the Pacific Ocean.

Competitive advantage	Competitive advantage occurs when an organization acquires or develops an attribute or combination of attributes that allows it to outperform its competitors. These attributes can include access to natural resources, such as high grade ores or inexpensive power, or access to highly trained and skilled personnel human resources. New technologies such as robotics and information technology can provide competitive advantage, whether as a part of the product itself, as an advantage to the making of the product, or as a competitive aid in the business process (for example, better identification and understanding of customers).
Industrial organization	In economics, industrial organization is a field that builds on the theory of the firm by examining the structure of firms and markets. Industrial organization adds real-world complications to the perfectly competitive model, complications such as transaction costs, limited information, and barriers to entry of new firms that may be associated with imperfect competition. It analyzes determinants of firm and market organization and behavior as between competition and monopoly, including from government actions.
Resource-based view	The resource-based view as a basis for the competitive advantage of a firm lies primarily in the application of a bundle of valuable tangible or intangible resources at the firm's disposal (Mwailu & Mercer, 1983 p142, Wernerfelt, 1984, p172; Rumelt, 1984, p557-558; Penrose, 1959). To transform a short-run competitive advantage into a sustained competitive advantage requires that these resources are heterogeneous in nature and not perfectly mobile (: p105-106; Peteraf, 1993, p180). Effectively, this translates into valuable resources that are neither perfectly imitable nor substitutable without great effort (Barney, 1991;: p117).
Cost	In production, research, retail, and accounting, a cost is the value of money that has been used up to produce something, and hence is not available for use anymore. In business, the cost may be one of acquisition, in which case the amount of money expended to acquire it is counted as cost. In this case, money is the input that is gone in order to acquire the thing.
Cost curve	In economics, a cost curve is a graph of the costs of production as a function of total quantity produced. In a free market economy, productively efficient firms use these curves to find the optimal point of production (minimizing cost), and profit maximizing firms can use them to decide output quantities to achieve those aims. There are various types of cost curves, all related to each other, including total and average cost curves, and marginal ('for each additional unit') cost curves, which are equal to the differential of the total cost curves.
Internet	The Internet is a global system of interconnected computer networks that use the standard Internet protocol suite to link several billion devices worldwide. It is a network of networks that consists of millions of private, public, academic, business, and government networks, of local to global scope, that are linked by a broad array of electronic, wireless, and optical networking technologies.

10. Strategy: The Quest to Keep Profit from Eroding

Product differentiation	In economics and marketing, product differentiation is the process of distinguishing a product or service from others, to make it more attractive to a particular target market. This involves differentiating it from competitors' products as well as a firm's own products. The concept was proposed by Edward Chamberlin in his 1933 Theory of Monopolistic Competition.
Adverse selection	Adverse selection, anti-selection, or negative selection is a term used in economics, insurance, risk management, and statistics. It refers to a market process in which undesired results occur when buyers and sellers have asymmetric information (access to different information); the 'bad' products or services are more likely to be selected. For example, a bank that sets one price for all of its checking account customers runs the risk of being adversely selected against by its low-balance, high-activity (and hence least profitable) customers.
Economies of scale	In microeconomics, economies of scale are the cost advantages that enterprises obtain due to size, output, or scale of operation, with cost per unit of output generally decreasing with increasing scale as fixed costs are spread out over more units of output. Often operational efficiency is also greater with increasing scale, leading to lower variable cost as well. Economies of scale apply to a variety of organizational and business situations and at various levels, such as a business or manufacturing unit, plant or an entire enterprise.

1. In economics, a _____ is a graph of the costs of production as a function of total quantity produced. In a free market economy, productively efficient firms use these curves to find the optimal point of production (minimizing cost), and profit maximizing firms can use them to decide output quantities to achieve those aims. There are various types of _____s, all related to each other, including total and average _____s, and marginal ('for each additional unit') _____s, which are equal to the differential of the total _____s.

   a. Beveridge curve
   b. Cost curve
   c. Contract curve
   d. Preference-rank translation

2. . The _____ family were a group of whalers based in Nantucket, Massachusetts, United States, from the seventeenth to the nineteenth centuries. Some members of the family gained wider exposure due to their discovery of various islands in the Pacific Ocean.

a. Starbuck

b. Coffin

c. Diogo da Rocha

d. Domingo de Bonechea

3. A _____ (from Greek monos μ???? + polein p??e?? (to sell)) exists when a specific person or enterprise is the only supplier of a particular commodity (this contrasts with a monopsony which relates to a single entity's control of a market to purchase a good or service, and with oligopoly which consists of a few entities dominating an industry). _____(ies) are thus characterized by a lack of economic competition to produce the good or service and a lack of viable substitute goods. The verb 'monopolize' refers to the process by which a company gains the ability to raise prices or exclude competitors.

a. Monopoly

b. Convertible husbandry

c. Corn exchange

d. Community-supported agriculture

4. In production, research, retail, and accounting, a _____ is the value of money that has been used up to produce something, and hence is not available for use anymore. In business, the _____ may be one of acquisition, in which case the amount of money expended to acquire it is counted as _____. In this case, money is the input that is gone in order to acquire the thing.

a. Cost

b. Federal Reserve

c. Fuel protests in the United Kingdom

d. 2010 student protest in Dublin

5. The _____ as a basis for the competitive advantage of a firm lies primarily in the application of a bundle of valuable tangible or intangible resources at the firm's disposal (Mwailu & Mercer, 1983 p142, Wernerfelt, 1984, p172; Rumelt, 1984, p557-558; Penrose, 1959). To transform a short-run competitive advantage into a sustained competitive advantage requires that these resources are heterogeneous in nature and not perfectly mobile (: p105-106; Peteraf, 1993, p180). Effectively, this translates into valuable resources that are neither perfectly imitable nor substitutable without great effort (Barney, 1991;: p117).

a. 6-3-5 Brainwriting

b. Resource-based view

c. Cambashi

d. Central location test

1. b

2. a

3. a

4. a

5. b

You can take the complete Chapter Practice Test

for 10. Strategy: The Quest to Keep Profit from Eroding
on all key terms, persons, places, and concepts.

Online 99 Cents

http://www.JustTheFacts101.com

Use www.JustTheFacts101.com for all your study needs

including Facts101's online interactive problem solving labs in

chemistry, statistics, mathematics, and more.

11. Foreign Exchange, Trade, and Bubbles

	Exchange rate
	Market
	Demand
	Devaluation
	Elasticity
	Exchange
	Great Moderation
	Home
	Renting
	Arbitrage
	Purchasing power
	Purchasing power parity

Exchange rate	European Monetary System was an arrangement established in 1979 under the Jenkins European Commission where most nations of the European Economic Community (EEC) linked their currencies to prevent large fluctuations relative to one another. After the demise of the Bretton Woods system in 1971, most of the EEC countries agreed in 1972 to maintain stable exchange rates by preventing exchange rate fluctuations of more than 2.25% (the European 'currency snake'). In March 1979, this system was replaced by the European Monetary System, and the European Currency Unit (ECU) was defined.
Market	A market is one of the many varieties of systems, institutions, procedures, social relations and infrastructures whereby parties engage in exchange.

	While parties may exchange goods and services by barter, most markets rely on sellers offering their goods or services (including labor) in exchange for money from buyers. It can be said that a market is the process by which the prices of goods and services are established.
Demand	In economics, demand for a good or service is an entire listing of the quantity of the good or service that a market would choose to buy, for every possible market price of the good or service. (Note: This distinguishes 'demand' from 'quantity demanded', where demand is a listing or graphing of quantity demanded at each possible price. In contrast to demand, quantity demanded is the exact quantity demanded at a certain price.
Devaluation	Devaluation in modern monetary policy is a reduction in the value of a currency with respect to those goods, services or other monetary units with which that currency can be exchanged. 'Devaluation' means official lowering of the value of a country's currency within a fixed exchange rate system, by which the monetary authority formally sets a new fixed rate with respect to a foreign reference currency. In contrast, depreciation is used to describe a decrease in a currency's value (relative to other major currency benchmarks) due to market forces, not government or central bank policy actions.
Elasticity	In economics, elasticity is the measurement of how responsive an economic variable is to a change in another. For example:•'If I lower the price of my product, how much more will I sell?'•'If I raise the price of one good, how will that affect sales of this other good?'•'If we learn that a resource is becoming scarce, will people scramble to acquire it?' An elastic variable (or elasticity value greater than 1) is one which responds more than proportionally to changes in other variables. In contrast, an inelastic variable (or elasticity value less than 1) is one which changes less than proportionally in response to changes in other variables.
Exchange	An exchange, or bourse, is a highly organized market where tradable securities, commodities, foreign exchange, futures, and options contracts are sold and bought.
Great Moderation	In economics, the Great Moderation refers to a reduction in the volatility of business cycle fluctuations starting in the mid-1980s, believed to have been caused by institutional and structural changes in developed nations in the later part of the twentieth century. Sometime during the mid-1980s major economic variables such as real gross domestic product growth, industrial production, monthly payroll employment and the unemployment rate began to decline in volatility.
Home	A home is a dwelling-place used as a permanent or semi-permanent residence for an individual, family, household or several families in a tribe. It is often a house, apartment, or other building, or alternatively a mobile home, houseboat, yurt or any other portable shelter. Larger groups may live in a nursing home, children's home, convent or any similar institution.

11. Foreign Exchange, Trade, and Bubbles

Renting	Renting, also known as hiring, is an agreement where a payment is made for the temporary use of a good, service or property owned by another. A gross lease is when the tenant pays a flat rental amount and the landlord pays for all property charges regularly incurred by the ownership.
Arbitrage	In economics and finance, arbitrage --such as a bank or brokerage firm. The term is mainly applied to trading in financial instruments, such as bonds, stocks, derivatives, commodities and currencies.
Purchasing power	Purchasing power is the number of goods or services that can be purchased with a unit of currency. For example, if one had taken one unit of currency to a store in the 1950s, it is probable that it would have been possible to buy a greater number of items than would today, indicating that one would have had a greater purchasing power in the 1950s. Currency can be either a commodity money, like gold or silver, or fiat currency, or free-floating market-valued currency like US dollars.
Purchasing power parity	Purchasing power parity is a component of some economic theories and is a technique used to determine the relative value of different currencies.
	Theories that invoke purchasing power parity assume that in some circumstances (for example, as a long-run tendency) it would cost exactly the same number of, say, US dollars to buy euros and then to use the proceeds to buy a market basket of goods as it would cost to use those dollars directly in purchasing the market basket of goods.
	The concept of purchasing power parity allows one to estimate what the exchange rate between two currencies would have to be in order for the exchange to be at par with the purchasing power of the two countries' currencies.

1. . European Monetary System was an arrangement established in 1979 under the Jenkins European Commission where most nations of the European Economic Community (EEC) linked their currencies to prevent large fluctuations relative to one another.

   After the demise of the Bretton Woods system in 1971, most of the EEC countries agreed in 1972 to maintain stable _____s by preventing _____ fluctuations of more than 2.25% (the European 'currency snake'). In March 1979, this system was replaced by the European Monetary System, and the European Currency Unit (ECU) was defined.

   a. Backsourcing
   b. Development aid
   c. Exchange rate

2. _____, also known as hiring, is an agreement where a payment is made for the temporary use of a good, service or property owned by another. A gross lease is when the tenant pays a flat rental amount and the landlord pays for all property charges regularly incurred by the ownership.

    a. Cigar Box Method
    b. Cash crop
    c. Renting
    d. CAPRI model

3. A _____ is one of the many varieties of systems, institutions, procedures, social relations and infrastructures whereby parties engage in exchange. While parties may exchange goods and services by barter, most _____s rely on sellers offering their goods or services (including labor) in exchange for money from buyers. It can be said that a _____ is the process by which the prices of goods and services are established.

    a. Contract farming
    b. Convertible husbandry
    c. Market
    d. Community-supported agriculture

4. _____ is the number of goods or services that can be purchased with a unit of currency. For example, if one had taken one unit of currency to a store in the 1950s, it is probable that it would have been possible to buy a greater number of items than would today, indicating that one would have had a greater _____ in the 1950s. Currency can be either a commodity money, like gold or silver, or fiat currency, or free-floating market-valued currency like US dollars.

    a. Belief
    b. Purchasing power
    c. Biological determination
    d. Causation

5. In economics, _____ for a good or service is an entire listing of the quantity of the good or service that a market would choose to buy, for every possible market price of the good or service. (Note: This distinguishes '_____' from 'quantity demanded', where _____ is a listing or graphing of quantity demanded at each possible price. In contrast to _____, quantity demanded is the exact quantity demanded at a certain price.

    a. Contract farming
    b. Demand
    c. Corn exchange
    d. Community-supported agriculture

1. c
2. c
3. c
4. b
5. b

You can take the complete Chapter Practice Test

for 11. Foreign Exchange, Trade, and Bubbles
on all key terms, persons, places, and concepts.

Online 99 Cents

http://www.JustTheFacts101.com

Use www.JustTheFacts101.com for all your study needs

including Facts101's online interactive problem solving labs in

chemistry, statistics, mathematics, and more.

12. More Realistic and Complex Pricing

	Cannibalization
	Present value
	Cost curve
	Yield management
	Yield
	Elasticity
	Psychological pricing
	Advertising
	Demand
	Prospect theory
	Fixed cost

CHAPTER HIGHLIGHTS & NOTES: KEY TERMS, PEOPLE, PLACES, CONCEPTS

Cannibalization	In marketing strategy, cannibalization refers to a reduction in sales volume, sales revenue, or market share of one product as a result of the introduction of a new product by the same producer.
	While this may seem inherently negative, in the context of a carefully planned strategy, it can be effective, by ultimately growing the market, or better meeting consumer demands. Cannibalization is a key consideration in product portfolio analysis.
Present value	Present value, also known as present discounted value, is a future amount of money that has been discounted to reflect its current value, as if it existed today. The present value is always less than or equal to the future value because money has interest-earning potential, a characteristic referred to as the time value of money. Time value can be described with the simplified phrase, "A dollar today is worth more than a dollar tomorrow".

Cost curve	In economics, a cost curve is a graph of the costs of production as a function of total quantity produced. In a free market economy, productively efficient firms use these curves to find the optimal point of production (minimizing cost), and profit maximizing firms can use them to decide output quantities to achieve those aims. There are various types of cost curves, all related to each other, including total and average cost curves, and marginal ('for each additional unit') cost curves, which are equal to the differential of the total cost curves.
Yield management	Yield management is a variable pricing strategy, based on understanding, anticipating and influencing consumer behavior in order to maximize revenue or profits from a fixed, perishable resource . As a specific, inventory-focused branch of revenue management, yield management involves strategic control of inventory to sell it to the right customer at the right time for the right price. This process can result in price discrimination, where a firm charges customers consuming otherwise identical goods or services a different price for doing so.
Yield	In finance, the term yield describes the amount in cash that returns to the owners of a security. Normally, it does not include the price variations, at the difference of the total return. Yield applies to various stated rates of return on stocks (common and preferred, and convertible), fixed income instruments (bonds, notes, bills, strips, zero coupon), and some other investment type insurance products (e.g. annuities).
Elasticity	In economics, elasticity is the measurement of how responsive an economic variable is to a change in another. For example:•'If I lower the price of my product, how much more will I sell?'•'If I raise the price of one good, how will that affect sales of this other good?'•'If we learn that a resource is becoming scarce, will people scramble to acquire it?' An elastic variable (or elasticity value greater than 1) is one which responds more than proportionally to changes in other variables. In contrast, an inelastic variable (or elasticity value less than 1) is one which changes less than proportionally in response to changes in other variables.
Psychological pricing	Psychological pricing is a pricing/marketing strategy based on the theory that certain prices have a psychological impact. The retail prices are often expressed as 'odd prices': a little less than a round number, e.g. $19.99 or £2.98. Consumers tend to perceive "odd prices" as being significantly lower than they actually are, tending to round to the next lowest monetary unit. Thus, prices such as $1.99 is associated with spending $1 rather than $2. The theory that drives this is that lower pricing such as this institutes greater demand than if consumers were perfectly rational.
Advertising	Advertising or advertizing in business is a form of marketing communication used to encourage, persuade, or manipulate an audience to take or continue to take some action. Most commonly, the desired result is to drive consumer behavior with respect to a commercial offering, although political and ideological advertising is also common.

12. More Realistic and Complex Pricing

Demand	In economics, demand for a good or service is an entire listing of the quantity of the good or service that a market would choose to buy, for every possible market price of the good or service. (Note: This distinguishes 'demand' from 'quantity demanded', where demand is a listing or graphing of quantity demanded at each possible price. In contrast to demand, quantity demanded is the exact quantity demanded at a certain price.
Prospect theory	Prospect theory is a behavioral economic theory that describes the way people choose between probabilistic alternatives that involve risk, where the probabilities of outcomes are known. The theory states that people make decisions based on the potential value of losses and gains rather than the final outcome, and that people evaluate these losses and gains using certain heuristics. The model is descriptive: it tries to model real-life choices, rather than optimal decisions.
Fixed cost	In economics, fixed costs, indirect costs or overheads are business expenses that are not dependent on the level of goods or services produced by the business. They tend to be time-related, such as salaries or rents being paid per month, and are often referred to as overhead costs. This is in contrast to variable costs, which are volume-related (and are paid per quantity produced).

1. In marketing strategy, _____ refers to a reduction in sales volume, sales revenue, or market share of one product as a result of the introduction of a new product by the same producer.

   While this may seem inherently negative, in the context of a carefully planned strategy, it can be effective, by ultimately growing the market, or better meeting consumer demands. _____ is a key consideration in product portfolio analysis.

   a. Back to school
   b. Backward invention
   c. Cannibalization
   d. Bayesian inference in marketing

2. . _____, also known as present discounted value, is a future amount of money that has been discounted to reflect its current value, as if it existed today. The _____ is always less than or equal to the future value because money has interest-earning potential, a characteristic referred to as the time value of money. Time value can be described with the simplified phrase, "A dollar today is worth more than a dollar tomorrow".

   a. Present value
   b. Cash accumulation equation
   c. Cointegration

3. _____ is a pricing/marketing strategy based on the theory that certain prices have a psychological impact. The retail prices are often expressed as 'odd prices': a little less than a round number, e.g. $19.99 or £2.98. Consumers tend to perceive "odd prices" as being significantly lower than they actually are, tending to round to the next lowest monetary unit. Thus, prices such as $1.99 is associated with spending $1 rather than $2. The theory that drives this is that lower pricing such as this institutes greater demand than if consumers were perfectly rational.

   a. Behavioral operations research
   b. Psychological pricing
   c. Belief structure
   d. Binary decision

4. In economics, _____s, indirect costs or overheads are business expenses that are not dependent on the level of goods or services produced by the business. They tend to be time-related, such as salaries or rents being paid per month, and are often referred to as overhead costs. This is in contrast to variable costs, which are volume-related (and are paid per quantity produced).

   a. Fixed cost
   b. Cost
   c. Cost accounting
   d. Cost curve

5. In finance, the term _____ describes the amount in cash that returns to the owners of a security. Normally, it does not include the price variations, at the difference of the total return. _____ applies to various stated rates of return on stocks (common and preferred, and convertible), fixed income instruments (bonds, notes, bills, strips, zero coupon), and some other investment type insurance products (e.g. annuities).

   a. Bauer Financial
   b. Yield
   c. CBDC NORTIP
   d. Chartered Financial Planner

1. c

2. a

3. b

4. a

5. b

You can take the complete Chapter Practice Test

for 12. More Realistic and Complex Pricing
on all key terms, persons, places, and concepts.

Online 99 Cents

http://www.JustTheFacts101.com

Use www.JustTheFacts101.com for all your study needs

including Facts101's online interactive problem solving labs in

chemistry, statistics, mathematics, and more.

13. Direct Price Discrimination

_____	Price discrimination _____
_____	Profit _____
_____	Arbitrage _____
_____	Antitrust law _____
_____	Antitrust _____

Price discrimination	Price discrimination or price differentiation is a pricing strategy where identical or largely similar goods or services are transacted at different prices by the same provider in different markets or territories. Price differentiation is distinguished from product differentiation by the more substantial difference in production cost for the differently priced products involved in the latter strategy. Price differentiation essentially relies on the variation in the customers' willingness to pay.
Profit	In neoclassical microeconomic theory, the term profit has two related but distinct meanings. Economic profit is similar to accounting profit but smaller because it reflects the total opportunity costs (both explicit and implicit) of a venture to an investor. Normal profit refers to a situation in which the economic profit is zero.
Arbitrage	In economics and finance, arbitrage --such as a bank or brokerage firm. The term is mainly applied to trading in financial instruments, such as bonds, stocks, derivatives, commodities and currencies.
Antitrust law	Competition law is law that promotes or seeks to maintain market competition by regulating anti-competitive conduct by companies. Competition law is implemented through Public and Private Enforcement Competition law is known as antitrust law in the United States and anti-monopoly law in China and Russia. In previous years it has been known as trade practices law in the United Kingdom and Australia.
Antitrust	Competition law is law that promotes or seeks to maintain market competition by regulating anti-competitive conduct by companies.

13. Direct Price Discrimination

Competition law is known as antitrust law in the United States and anti-monopoly law in China and Russia. In previous years it has been known as trade practices law in the United Kingdom and Australia.

1. _____ or price differentiation is a pricing strategy where identical or largely similar goods or services are transacted at different prices by the same provider in different markets or territories. Price differentiation is distinguished from product differentiation by the more substantial difference in production cost for the differently priced products involved in the latter strategy. Price differentiation essentially relies on the variation in the customers' willingness to pay.

   a. Price discrimination
   b. Bliss point
   c. Club good
   d. Conjectural variation

2. In economics and finance, _____ --such as a bank or brokerage firm. The term is mainly applied to trading in financial instruments, such as bonds, stocks, derivatives, commodities and currencies.

   a. Financial market
   b. Market
   c. CAPRI model
   d. Arbitrage

3. In neoclassical microeconomic theory, the term _____ has two related but distinct meanings. Economic _____ is similar to accounting _____ but smaller because it reflects the total opportunity costs (both explicit and implicit) of a venture to an investor. Normal _____ refers to a situation in which the economic _____ is zero.

   a. Profit
   b. Bliss point
   c. Club good
   d. Conjectural variation

4. . Competition law is law that promotes or seeks to maintain market competition by regulating anti-competitive conduct by companies. Competition law is implemented through Public and Private Enforcement

   Competition law is known as _____ in the United States and anti-monopoly law in China and Russia. In previous years it has been known as trade practices law in the United Kingdom and Australia.

    a. Interstate Commerce Commission

    b. Market

    c. Antitrust law

    d. Casa grande

5. Competition law is law that promotes or seeks to maintain market competition by regulating anti-competitive conduct by companies.

Competition law is known as _____ law in the United States and anti-monopoly law in China and Russia. In previous years it has been known as trade practices law in the United Kingdom and Australia.

    a. Enterprise Act 2002

    b. Antitrust

    c. European Union competition law

    d. European Union merger law

1. a

2. d

3. a

4. c

5. b

You can take the complete Chapter Practice Test

for 13. Direct Price Discrimination
on all key terms, persons, places, and concepts.

Online 99 Cents

http://www.JustTheFacts101.com

Use www.JustTheFacts101.com for all your study needs

including Facts101's online interactive problem solving labs in

chemistry, statistics, mathematics, and more.

14. Indirect Price Discrimination

CHAPTER OUTLINE: KEY TERMS, PEOPLE, PLACES, CONCEPTS

	Adobe
	Present value
	Price discrimination
	Profit
	Cannibalization
	Bundling

CHAPTER HIGHLIGHTS & NOTES: KEY TERMS, PEOPLE, PLACES, CONCEPTS

Adobe	Adobe is the Spanish word for mud brick, a natural building material made from sand, clay, water, and some kind of fibrous or organic material (sticks, straw, and/or manure), usually shaped into bricks using molds and dried in the sun. Adobe buildings are similar to cob and rammed earth buildings, but cob and rammed earth are directly made into walls rather than bricks. The Romanian name for this material is chirpici.
Present value	Present value, also known as present discounted value, is a future amount of money that has been discounted to reflect its current value, as if it existed today. The present value is always less than or equal to the future value because money has interest-earning potential, a characteristic referred to as the time value of money. Time value can be described with the simplified phrase, "A dollar today is worth more than a dollar tomorrow".
Price discrimination	Price discrimination or price differentiation is a pricing strategy where identical or largely similar goods or services are transacted at different prices by the same provider in different markets or territories. Price differentiation is distinguished from product differentiation by the more substantial difference in production cost for the differently priced products involved in the latter strategy. Price differentiation essentially relies on the variation in the customers' willingness to pay.
Profit	In neoclassical microeconomic theory, the term profit has two related but distinct meanings. Economic profit is similar to accounting profit but smaller because it reflects the total opportunity costs (both explicit and implicit) of a venture to an investor. Normal profit refers to a situation in which the economic profit is zero.

14. Indirect Price Discrimination

Cannibalization	In marketing strategy, cannibalization refers to a reduction in sales volume, sales revenue, or market share of one product as a result of the introduction of a new product by the same producer.
	While this may seem inherently negative, in the context of a carefully planned strategy, it can be effective, by ultimately growing the market, or better meeting consumer demands. Cannibalization is a key consideration in product portfolio analysis.
Bundling	In political science and public choice theory, bundling is a concept used for studying the selection of candidates for public office. A voter typically chooses a candidate (or party) for the legislature, rather than directly voting for specific policies. When doing so, the voter is essentially selecting among bundles of policies that a candidate or a party will enact if in power.

1. _____ is the Spanish word for mud brick, a natural building material made from sand, clay, water, and some kind of fibrous or organic material (sticks, straw, and/or manure), usually shaped into bricks using molds and dried in the sun. _____ buildings are similar to cob and rammed earth buildings, but cob and rammed earth are directly made into walls rather than bricks. The Romanian name for this material is chirpici.

    a. Fuel protests in the United Kingdom
    b. Battle of Annaberg
    c. Freikorps Lichtschlag
    d. Adobe

2. In marketing strategy, _____ refers to a reduction in sales volume, sales revenue, or market share of one product as a result of the introduction of a new product by the same producer.

    While this may seem inherently negative, in the context of a carefully planned strategy, it can be effective, by ultimately growing the market, or better meeting consumer demands. _____ is a key consideration in product portfolio analysis.

    a. Cannibalization
    b. Backward invention
    c. Bass diffusion model
    d. Bayesian inference in marketing

3. . _____, also known as present discounted value, is a future amount of money that has been discounted to reflect its current value, as if it existed today. The _____ is always less than or equal to the future value because money has interest-earning potential, a characteristic referred to as the time value of money.

Time value can be described with the simplified phrase, "A dollar today is worth more than a dollar tomorrow".

a. Bond equivalent yield
b. Cash accumulation equation
c. Cointegration
d. Present value

4. _____ or price differentiation is a pricing strategy where identical or largely similar goods or services are transacted at different prices by the same provider in different markets or territories. Price differentiation is distinguished from product differentiation by the more substantial difference in production cost for the differently priced products involved in the latter strategy. Price differentiation essentially relies on the variation in the customers' willingness to pay.

a. Benefit principle
b. Bliss point
c. Price discrimination
d. Conjectural variation

5. In neoclassical microeconomic theory, the term _____ has two related but distinct meanings. Economic _____ is similar to accounting _____ but smaller because it reflects the total opportunity costs (both explicit and implicit) of a venture to an investor. Normal _____ refers to a situation in which the economic _____ is zero.

a. Profit
b. Bliss point
c. Club good
d. Conjectural variation

1. d

2. a

3. d

4. c

5. a

You can take the complete Chapter Practice Test

for 14. Indirect Price Discrimination
on all key terms, persons, places, and concepts.

Online 99 Cents

http://www.JustTheFacts101.com

Use www.JustTheFacts101.com for all your study needs

including Facts101's online interactive problem solving labs in

chemistry, statistics, mathematics, and more.

15. Strategic Games

	Nash equilibrium
	Prisoner's dilemma
	Price discrimination
	Price
	First-mover advantage
	Michelin

CHAPTER HIGHLIGHTS & NOTES: KEY TERMS, PEOPLE, PLACES, CONCEPTS

Nash equilibrium	In game theory, the Nash equilibrium is a solution concept of a non-cooperative game involving two or more players, in which each player is assumed to know the equilibrium strategies of the other players, and no player has anything to gain by changing only their own strategy. If each player has chosen a strategy and no player can benefit by changing strategies while the other players keep theirs unchanged, then the current set of strategy choices and the corresponding payoffs constitute a Nash equilibrium. Stated simply, Amy and Wili are in Nash equilibrium if Amy is making the best decision she can, taking into account Wili's decision, and Wili is making the best decision he can, taking into account Amy's decision.
Prisoner's dilemma	The prisoner's dilemma is a canonical example of a game analyzed in game theory that shows why two purely 'rational' individuals might not cooperate, even if it appears that it is in their best interests to do so. It was originally framed by Merrill Flood and Melvin Dresher working at RAND in 1950. Albert W. Tucker formalized the game with prison sentence rewards and gave it the name 'prisoner's dilemma' (Poundstone, 1992), presenting it as follows:Two members of a criminal gang are arrested and imprisoned. Each prisoner is in solitary confinement with no means of speaking to or exchanging messages with the other.
Price discrimination	Price discrimination or price differentiation is a pricing strategy where identical or largely similar goods or services are transacted at different prices by the same provider in different markets or territories. Price differentiation is distinguished from product differentiation by the more substantial difference in production cost for the differently priced products involved in the latter strategy.

Price	In ordinary usage, price is the quantity of payment or compensation given by one party to another in return for goods or services.
	In modern economies, prices are generally expressed in units of some form of currency. (For commodities, they are expressed as currency per unit weight of the commodity, e.g. euros per kilogram).
First-mover advantage	In business, economics, or marketing, first-mover advantage, or First mover advantage, is the advantage gained by the initial significant occupant of a market segment. It may be also referred to as Technological Leadership. This advantage may stem from the fact that the first entrant can gain control of resources that followers may not be able to match.
Michelin	Michelin is a tyre manufacturer based in Clermont-Ferrand in the Auvergne région of France. It is one of the two largest tyre manufacturers in the world along with Bridgestone. In addition to the Michelin brand, it also owns the BFGoodrich, Kleber, Tigar, Riken, Kormoran and Uniroyal (in North America) tyre brands.

1. The _____ is a canonical example of a game analyzed in game theory that shows why two purely 'rational' individuals might not cooperate, even if it appears that it is in their best interests to do so. It was originally framed by Merrill Flood and Melvin Dresher working at RAND in 1950. Albert W. Tucker formalized the game with prison sentence rewards and gave it the name '_____' (Poundstone, 1992), presenting it as follows:Two members of a criminal gang are arrested and imprisoned. Each prisoner is in solitary confinement with no means of speaking to or exchanging messages with the other.

   a. Gresham's Law
   b. Backward induction
   c. Bandwidth-sharing game
   d. Prisoner's dilemma

2. . In game theory, the _____ is a solution concept of a non-cooperative game involving two or more players, in which each player is assumed to know the equilibrium strategies of the other players, and no player has anything to gain by changing only their own strategy. If each player has chosen a strategy and no player can benefit by changing strategies while the other players keep theirs unchanged, then the current set of strategy choices and the corresponding payoffs constitute a _____.

   Stated simply, Amy and Wili are in _____ if Amy is making the best decision she can, taking into account Wili's decision, and Wili is making the best decision he can, taking into account Amy's decision.

   a. Nash equilibrium

b. Backward induction

c. Bandwidth-sharing game

d. Bayesian efficiency

3. _____ or price differentiation is a pricing strategy where identical or largely similar goods or services are transacted at different prices by the same provider in different markets or territories. Price differentiation is distinguished from product differentiation by the more substantial difference in production cost for the differently priced products involved in the latter strategy. Price differentiation essentially relies on the variation in the customers' willingness to pay.

a. Benefit principle

b. Bliss point

c. Price discrimination

d. Conjectural variation

4. In ordinary usage, _____ is the quantity of payment or compensation given by one party to another in return for goods or services.

   In modern economies, _____s are generally expressed in units of some form of currency. (For commodities, they are expressed as currency per unit weight of the commodity, e.g. euros per kilogram).

a. Price

b. Backward invention

c. Bass diffusion model

d. Bayesian inference in marketing

5. In business, economics, or marketing, _____, or First mover advantage, is the advantage gained by the initial significant occupant of a market segment. It may be also referred to as Technological Leadership. This advantage may stem from the fact that the first entrant can gain control of resources that followers may not be able to match.

a. Back office

b. Balanced scorecard

c. Bestshoring

d. First-mover advantage

1. d
2. a
3. c
4. a
5. d

You can take the complete Chapter Practice Test

for 15. Strategic Games
on all key terms, persons, places, and concepts.

Online 99 Cents

http://www.JustTheFacts101.com

Use www.JustTheFacts101.com for all your study needs

including Facts101's online interactive problem solving labs in

chemistry, statistics, mathematics, and more.

16. Bargaining

CHAPTER OUTLINE: KEY TERMS, PEOPLE, PLACES, CONCEPTS

	First-mover advantage
	Cost curve
	Nash equilibrium
	Opportunity cost
	Managed care

CHAPTER HIGHLIGHTS & NOTES: KEY TERMS, PEOPLE, PLACES, CONCEPTS

First-mover advantage	In business, economics, or marketing, first-mover advantage, or First mover advantage, is the advantage gained by the initial significant occupant of a market segment. It may be also referred to as Technological Leadership. This advantage may stem from the fact that the first entrant can gain control of resources that followers may not be able to match.
Cost curve	In economics, a cost curve is a graph of the costs of production as a function of total quantity produced. In a free market economy, productively efficient firms use these curves to find the optimal point of production (minimizing cost), and profit maximizing firms can use them to decide output quantities to achieve those aims. There are various types of cost curves, all related to each other, including total and average cost curves, and marginal ('for each additional unit') cost curves, which are equal to the differential of the total cost curves.
Nash equilibrium	In game theory, the Nash equilibrium is a solution concept of a non-cooperative game involving two or more players, in which each player is assumed to know the equilibrium strategies of the other players, and no player has anything to gain by changing only their own strategy. If each player has chosen a strategy and no player can benefit by changing strategies while the other players keep theirs unchanged, then the current set of strategy choices and the corresponding payoffs constitute a Nash equilibrium.

Stated simply, Amy and Wili are in Nash equilibrium if Amy is making the best decision she can, taking into account Wili's decision, and Wili is making the best decision he can, taking into account Amy's decision. |

16. Bargaining

Opportunity cost	In microeconomic theory, the opportunity cost of a choice is the value of the best alternative forgone, in a situation in which a choice needs to be made between several mutually exclusive alternatives given limited resources. Assuming the best choice is made, it is the 'cost' incurred by not enjoying the benefit that would be had by taking the second best choice available. The New Oxford American Dictionary defines it as 'the loss of potential gain from other alternatives when one alternative is chosen'.
Managed care	The term managed care or managed health care is used in the United States to describe a variety of techniques intended to reduce the cost of providing health benefits and improve the quality of care ('managed care techniques'), for organizations that use those techniques or provide them as services to other organizations ('managed care organization' or 'MCO'), or to describe systems of financing and delivering health care to enrollees organized around managed care techniques and concepts ('managed care delivery systems').

...intended to reduce unnecessary health care costs through a variety of mechanisms, including: economic incentives for physicians and patients to select less costly forms of care; programs for reviewing the medical necessity of specific services; increased beneficiary cost sharing; controls on inpatient admissions and lengths of stay; the establishment of cost-sharing incentives for outpatient surgery; selective contracting with health care providers; and the intensive management of high-cost health care cases. The programs may be provided in a variety of settings, such as Health Maintenance Organizations and Preferred Provider Organizations. |

1. In business, economics, or marketing, _____, or First mover advantage, is the advantage gained by the initial significant occupant of a market segment. It may be also referred to as Technological Leadership. This advantage may stem from the fact that the first entrant can gain control of resources that followers may not be able to match.

   a. Back office
   b. Balanced scorecard
   c. Bestshoring
   d. First-mover advantage

2. . In economics, a _____ is a graph of the costs of production as a function of total quantity produced. In a free market economy, productively efficient firms use these curves to find the optimal point of production (minimizing cost), and profit maximizing firms can use them to decide output quantities to achieve those aims. There are various types of _____s, all related to each other, including total and average _____s, and marginal ('for each additional unit') _____s, which are equal to the differential of the total _____s.

a. Beveridge curve
b. Budget constraint
c. Contract curve
d. Cost curve

3. In microeconomic theory, the _____ of a choice is the value of the best alternative forgone, in a situation in which a choice needs to be made between several mutually exclusive alternatives given limited resources. Assuming the best choice is made, it is the 'cost' incurred by not enjoying the benefit that would be had by taking the second best choice available. The New Oxford American Dictionary defines it as 'the loss of potential gain from other alternatives when one alternative is chosen'.

a. Benefit principle
b. Bliss point
c. Club good
d. Opportunity cost

4. In game theory, the _____ is a solution concept of a non-cooperative game involving two or more players, in which each player is assumed to know the equilibrium strategies of the other players, and no player has anything to gain by changing only their own strategy. If each player has chosen a strategy and no player can benefit by changing strategies while the other players keep theirs unchanged, then the current set of strategy choices and the corresponding payoffs constitute a _____.

Stated simply, Amy and Wili are in _____ if Amy is making the best decision she can, taking into account Wili's decision, and Wili is making the best decision he can, taking into account Amy's decision.

a. Backgammon opening theory
b. Backward induction
c. Nash equilibrium
d. Bayesian efficiency

5. . The term _____ or managed health care is used in the United States to describe a variety of techniques intended to reduce the cost of providing health benefits and improve the quality of care ('_____ techniques'), for organizations that use those techniques or provide them as services to other organizations ('_____ organization' or 'MCO'), or to describe systems of financing and delivering health care to enrollees organized around _____ techniques and concepts ('_____ delivery systems'). '

...intended to reduce unnecessary health care costs through a variety of mechanisms, including: economic incentives for physicians and patients to select less costly forms of care; programs for reviewing the medical necessity of specific services; increased beneficiary cost sharing; controls on inpatient admissions and lengths of stay; the establishment of cost-sharing incentives for outpatient surgery; selective contracting with health care providers; and the intensive management of high-cost health care cases. The programs may be provided in a variety of settings, such as Health Maintenance Organizations and Preferred Provider Organizations.'

16. Bargaining

a. Bituah Leumi
b. Boiler insurance
c. Business owner%27s policy
d. Managed care

1. d
2. d
3. d
4. c
5. d

You can take the complete Chapter Practice Test

for 16. Bargaining
on all key terms, persons, places, and concepts.

Online 99 Cents

http://www.JustTheFacts101.com

Use www.JustTheFacts101.com for all your study needs

including Facts101's online interactive problem solving labs in

chemistry, statistics, mathematics, and more.

CHAPTER OUTLINE: KEY TERMS, PEOPLE, PLACES, CONCEPTS

	Random variable
	Prisoner's dilemma
	Variable
	Adobe
	Cost
	Price discrimination
	Experiment
	Cost curve
	Google

CHAPTER HIGHLIGHTS & NOTES: KEY TERMS, PEOPLE, PLACES, CONCEPTS

| Random variable | In probability and statistics, a random variable, aleatory variable or stochastic variable is a variable whose value is subject to variations due to chance . A random variable can take on a set of possible different values (similarly to other mathematical variables), each with an associated probability (if discrete) or a probability density function (if continuous), in contrast to other mathematical variables.

A random variable's possible values might represent the possible outcomes of a yet-to-be-performed experiment, or the possible outcomes of a past experiment whose already-existing value is uncertain (for example, as a result of incomplete information or imprecise measurements). |
|---|---|
| Prisoner's dilemma | The prisoner's dilemma is a canonical example of a game analyzed in game theory that shows why two purely 'rational' individuals might not cooperate, even if it appears that it is in their best interests to do so. It was originally framed by Merrill Flood and Melvin Dresher working at RAND in 1950. Albert W. Tucker formalized the game with prison sentence rewards and gave it the name 'prisoner's dilemma' (Poundstone, 1992), presenting it as follows:Two members of a criminal gang are arrested and imprisoned. |

17. Making Decisions with Uncertainty

Variable	In elementary mathematics, a variable is an alphabetic character representing a number which is either arbitrary or not fully specified or unknown. Making algebraic computations with variables as if they were explicit numbers allows one to solve a range of problems in a single computation. A typical example is the quadratic formula, which allows to solve every quadratic equation by simply substituting the numeric values of the coefficients of the given equation to the variables that represent them.
Adobe	Adobe is the Spanish word for mud brick, a natural building material made from sand, clay, water, and some kind of fibrous or organic material (sticks, straw, and/or manure), usually shaped into bricks using molds and dried in the sun. Adobe buildings are similar to cob and rammed earth buildings, but cob and rammed earth are directly made into walls rather than bricks. The Romanian name for this material is chirpici.
Cost	In production, research, retail, and accounting, a cost is the value of money that has been used up to produce something, and hence is not available for use anymore. In business, the cost may be one of acquisition, in which case the amount of money expended to acquire it is counted as cost. In this case, money is the input that is gone in order to acquire the thing.
Price discrimination	Price discrimination or price differentiation is a pricing strategy where identical or largely similar goods or services are transacted at different prices by the same provider in different markets or territories. Price differentiation is distinguished from product differentiation by the more substantial difference in production cost for the differently priced products involved in the latter strategy. Price differentiation essentially relies on the variation in the customers' willingness to pay.
Experiment	An experiment is an orderly procedure carried out with the goal of verifying, refuting, or establishing the validity of a hypothesis. Controlled experiments provide insight into cause-and-effect by demonstrating what outcome occurs when a particular factor is manipulated. Controlled experiments vary greatly in their goal and scale, but always rely on repeatable procedure and logical analysis of the results.
Cost curve	In economics, a cost curve is a graph of the costs of production as a function of total quantity produced. In a free market economy, productively efficient firms use these curves to find the optimal point of production (minimizing cost), and profit maximizing firms can use them to decide output quantities to achieve those aims. There are various types of cost curves, all related to each other, including total and average cost curves, and marginal ('for each additional unit') cost curves, which are equal to the differential of the total cost curves.
Google	Google is an American multinational corporation specializing in Internet-related services and products. These include search, cloud computing, software, and online advertising technologies. Most of its profits are derived from AdWords.

1. An _____ is an orderly procedure carried out with the goal of verifying, refuting, or establishing the validity of a hypothesis. Controlled _____s provide insight into cause-and-effect by demonstrating what outcome occurs when a particular factor is manipulated. Controlled _____s vary greatly in their goal and scale, but always rely on repeatable procedure and logical analysis of the results.

   a. Bayesian experimental design
   b. Between-group design
   c. Block design
   d. Experiment

2. In probability and statistics, a _____, aleatory variable or stochastic variable is a variable whose value is subject to variations due to chance . A _____ can take on a set of possible different values (similarly to other mathematical variables), each with an associated probability (if discrete) or a probability density function (if continuous), in contrast to other mathematical variables.

   A _____'s possible values might represent the possible outcomes of a yet-to-be-performed experiment, or the possible outcomes of a past experiment whose already-existing value is uncertain (for example, as a result of incomplete information or imprecise measurements).

   a. Bias of an estimator
   b. Random variable
   c. Fisher transformation
   d. L-statistic

3. The _____ is a canonical example of a game analyzed in game theory that shows why two purely 'rational' individuals might not cooperate, even if it appears that it is in their best interests to do so. It was originally framed by Merrill Flood and Melvin Dresher working at RAND in 1950. Albert W. Tucker formalized the game with prison sentence rewards and gave it the name '_____' (Poundstone, 1992), presenting it as follows:Two members of a criminal gang are arrested and imprisoned. Each prisoner is in solitary confinement with no means of speaking to or exchanging messages with the other.

   a. Prisoner's dilemma
   b. Decoupling
   c. Fisher transformation
   d. L-statistic

4. . In elementary mathematics, a _____ is an alphabetic character representing a number which is either arbitrary or not fully specified or unknown. Making algebraic computations with _____s as if they were explicit numbers allows one to solve a range of problems in a single computation. A typical example is the quadratic formula, which allows to solve every quadratic equation by simply substituting the numeric values of the coefficients of the given equation to the _____s that represent them.

   a. Cause of death
   b. Ceiling effect

    c. Central limit theorem

    d. Variable

5. _____ is an American multinational corporation specializing in Internet-related services and products. These include search, cloud computing, software, and online advertising technologies. Most of its profits are derived from AdWords.

    a. Backlink

    b. Blackstartup

    c. Google

    d. Chief web officer

1. d

2. b

3. a

4. d

5. c

You can take the complete Chapter Practice Test

for 17. Making Decisions with Uncertainty
on all key terms, persons, places, and concepts.

Online 99 Cents

http://www.JustTheFacts101.com

Use www.JustTheFacts101.com for all your study needs

including Facts101's online interactive problem solving labs in

chemistry, statistics, mathematics, and more.

18. Auctions

CHAPTER OUTLINE: KEY TERMS, PEOPLE, PLACES, CONCEPTS

	Auction
	English auction
	Bid rigging
	Cartel
	Collusion
	Google
	Backcasting
	Winner's curse

CHAPTER HIGHLIGHTS & NOTES: KEY TERMS, PEOPLE, PLACES, CONCEPTS

Auction	An auction is a process of buying and selling goods or services by offering them up for bid, taking bids, and then selling the item to the highest bidder. In economic theory, an auction may refer to any mechanism or set of trading rules for exchange.
English auction	An English auction is a type of auction, whose most typical form is the 'open outcry' auction. The auctioneer opens the auction by announcing a Suggested Opening Bid, a starting price or reserve for the item on sale and then accepts increasingly higher bids from the floor consisting of buyers with a possible interest in the item. Unlike sealed bid auctions, 'open outcry' auctions are 'open' or fully transparent as the identity of all bidders is disclosed to each other during the auction.
Bid rigging	Bid rigging is a form of fraud in which a commercial contract is promised to one party even though for the sake of appearance several other parties also present a bid. This form of collusion is illegal in most countries. It is a form of price fixing and market allocation, often practiced where contracts are determined by a call for bids, for example in the case of government construction contracts.
Cartel	A cartel is a formal 'agreement' among competing firms. It is a formal organization of producers and manufacturers that agree to fix prices, marketing, and production.

18. Auctions

Collusion	Collusion is an agreement between two or more parties, sometimes illegal and therefore secretive, to limit open competition by deceiving, misleading, or defrauding others of their legal rights, or to obtain an objective forbidden by law typically by defrauding or gaining an unfair advantage. It is an agreement among firms or individuals to divide a market, set prices, limit production or limit opportunities. It can involve 'wage fixing, kickbacks, or misrepresenting the independence of the relationship between the colluding parties'.
Google	Google is an American multinational corporation specializing in Internet-related services and products. These include search, cloud computing, software, and online advertising technologies. Most of its profits are derived from AdWords.
Backcasting	Backcasting starts with defining a desirable future and then works backwards to identify policies and programs that will connect the future to the present. The fundamental question of backcasting asks: 'if we want to attain a certain goal, what actions must be taken to get there?'Forecasting is the process of predicting the future based on current trend analysis. Backcasting approaches the challenge of discussing the future from the opposite direction.
Winner's curse	The winner's curse is a phenomenon that may occur in common value auctions with incomplete information. In short, the winner's curse says that in such an auction, the winner will tend to overpay. The winner may overpay or be 'cursed' in one of two ways: 1) the winning bid exceeds the value of the auctioned asset such that the winner is worse off in absolute terms; or 2) the value of the asset is less than the bidder anticipated, so the bidder may still have a net gain but will be worse off than anticipated.

1. An _____ is a type of auction, whose most typical form is the 'open outcry' auction. The auctioneer opens the auction by announcing a Suggested Opening Bid, a starting price or reserve for the item on sale and then accepts increasingly higher bids from the floor consisting of buyers with a possible interest in the item. Unlike sealed bid auctions, 'open outcry' auctions are 'open' or fully transparent as the identity of all bidders is disclosed to each other during the auction.

   a. English auction
   b. Bidding
   c. Bidding fee auction
   d. Bid-to-cover ratio

2. . An _____ is a process of buying and selling goods or services by offering them up for bid, taking bids, and then selling the item to the highest bidder. In economic theory, an _____ may refer to any mechanism or set of trading rules for exchange.

a. Auction

b. Daniel Kahneman

c. Base rate fallacy

d. Behavioral portfolio theory

3. _____ is a form of fraud in which a commercial contract is promised to one party even though for the sake of appearance several other parties also present a bid. This form of collusion is illegal in most countries. It is a form of price fixing and market allocation, often practiced where contracts are determined by a call for bids, for example in the case of government construction contracts.

a. Barriers to entry

b. Bathtub Trust

c. Fuel protests in the United Kingdom

d. Bid rigging

4. The _____ is a phenomenon that may occur in common value auctions with incomplete information. In short, the _____ says that in such an auction, the winner will tend to overpay. The winner may overpay or be 'cursed' in one of two ways: 1) the winning bid exceeds the value of the auctioned asset such that the winner is worse off in absolute terms; or 2) the value of the asset is less than the bidder anticipated, so the bidder may still have a net gain but will be worse off than anticipated.

a. Gresham's Law

b. Random matrix

c. Wick product

d. Winner's curse

5. A _____ is a formal 'agreement' among competing firms. It is a formal organization of producers and manufacturers that agree to fix prices, marketing, and production. _____s usually occur in an oligopolistic industry, where the number of sellers is small (usually because barriers to entry, most notably startup costs, are high) and the products being traded are usually commodities.

a. Common Agricultural Policy

b. Cartel

c. Community-supported agriculture

d. Contract farming

1. a
2. a
3. d
4. d
5. b

You can take the complete Chapter Practice Test

for 18. Auctions
on all key terms, persons, places, and concepts.

Online 99 Cents

http://www.JustTheFacts101.com

Use www.JustTheFacts101.com for all your study needs

including Facts101's online interactive problem solving labs in

chemistry, statistics, mathematics, and more.

19. The Problem of Adverse Selection

_____	Adobe
_____	Public offering
_____	Adverse selection
_____	Information asymmetry
_____	Initial public offering
_____	Winner's curse
_____	Screening
_____	Deductible
_____	Internet
_____	Online auction
_____	Sales

CHAPTER HIGHLIGHTS & NOTES: KEY TERMS, PEOPLE, PLACES, CONCEPTS

Adobe	Adobe is the Spanish word for mud brick, a natural building material made from sand, clay, water, and some kind of fibrous or organic material (sticks, straw, and/or manure), usually shaped into bricks using molds and dried in the sun. Adobe buildings are similar to cob and rammed earth buildings, but cob and rammed earth are directly made into walls rather than bricks. The Romanian name for this material is chirpici.
Public offering	A public offering is the offering of securities of a company or a similar corporation to the public. Generally, the securities are to be listed on a stock exchange. In most jurisdictions, a public offering requires the issuing company to publish a prospectus detailing the terms and rights attached to the offered security, as well as information on the company itself and its finances.
Adverse selection	Adverse selection, anti-selection, or negative selection is a term used in economics, insurance, risk management, and statistics.

It refers to a market process in which undesired results occur when buyers and sellers have asymmetric information (access to different information); the 'bad' products or services are more likely to be selected. For example, a bank that sets one price for all of its checking account customers runs the risk of being adversely selected against by its low-balance, high-activity (and hence least profitable) customers.

| Information asymmetry | In contract theory and economics, information asymmetry deals with the study of decisions in transactions where one party has more or better information than the other. In contrast to neo-classical economics which assumes perfect information, this is about 'What We Don't Know'. This creates an imbalance of power in transactions which can sometimes cause the transactions to go awry, a kind of market failure in the worst case. |

| Initial public offering | Initial public offering or stock market launch is a type of public offering where shares of stock in a company are sold to the general public, on a securities exchange, for the first time. Through this process, a private company transforms into a public company. Initial public offerings are used by companies to raise expansion capital, to possibly monetize the investments of early private investors, and to become publicly traded enterprises. |

| Winner's curse | The winner's curse is a phenomenon that may occur in common value auctions with incomplete information. In short, the winner's curse says that in such an auction, the winner will tend to overpay. The winner may overpay or be 'cursed' in one of two ways: 1) the winning bid exceeds the value of the auctioned asset such that the winner is worse off in absolute terms; or 2) the value of the asset is less than the bidder anticipated, so the bidder may still have a net gain but will be worse off than anticipated. |

| Screening | Screening in economics refers to a strategy of combating adverse selection, one of the potential decision-making complications in cases of asymmetric information. The concept of screening was first developed by Michael Spence (1973), and should be distinguished from signalling, which implies that the informed agent moves first.

For purposes of screening, asymmetric information cases assume two economic agents--which we call, for example, Abel and Cain--where Abel knows more about himself than Cain knows about Abel. |

| Deductible | In an insurance policy, the deductible is the amount of expenses that must be paid out of pocket before an insurer will pay any expenses. Example: if you have a $5000 deductible per year and you happen to spend $6000 this year, you will get your reimbursement for $1000 this year. In general usage, the term deductible may be used to describe one of several types of clauses that are used by insurance companies as a threshold for policy payments. |

| Internet | The Internet is a global system of interconnected computer networks that use the standard Internet protocol suite to link several billion devices worldwide. |

19. The Problem of Adverse Selection

	It is a network of networks that consists of millions of private, public, academic, business, and government networks, of local to global scope, that are linked by a broad array of electronic, wireless, and optical networking technologies. The Internet carries an extensive range of information resources and services, such as the inter-linked hypertext documents and applications of the World Wide Web (WWW), the infrastructure to support email, and peer-to-peer networks for file sharing and telephony.
Online auction	An online auction is an auction which is held over the internet. Online auctions come in many different formats, but most popularly they are ascending English auctions, descending Dutch auctions, first-price sealed-bid, Vickrey auctions, or sometimes even a combination of multiple auctions, taking elements of one and forging them with another. The scope and reach of these auctions have been propelled by the Internet to a level beyond what the initial purveyors had anticipated.
Sales	A sale is the act of selling a product or service in return for money or other compensation. Signalling completion of the prospective stage, it is the beginning of an engagement between customer and vendor or the extension of that engagement.
	The seller or salesperson - the provider of the goods or services - completes a sale in response to an acquisition or to an appropriation or to a request.

1. A _____ is the offering of securities of a company or a similar corporation to the public. Generally, the securities are to be listed on a stock exchange. In most jurisdictions, a _____ requires the issuing company to publish a prospectus detailing the terms and rights attached to the offered security, as well as information on the company itself and its finances.

    a. Bid price
    b. Big Bang
    c. Big boy letter
    d. Public offering

2. . The _____ is a global system of interconnected computer networks that use the standard _____ protocol suite to link several billion devices worldwide. It is a network of networks that consists of millions of private, public, academic, business, and government networks, of local to global scope, that are linked by a broad array of electronic, wireless, and optical networking technologies. The _____ carries an extensive range of information resources and services, such as the inter-linked hypertext documents and applications of the World Wide Web (WWW), the infrastructure to support email, and peer-to-peer networks for file sharing and telephony.

    a. Internet

b. Cultural homogenization

c. Democratization of technology

d. Global elite

3. A _____(es) is the act of selling a product or service in return for money or other compensation. Signalling completion of the prospective stage, it is the beginning of an engagement between customer and vendor or the extension of that engagement.

The seller or salesperson - the provider of the goods or services - completes a _____(es) in response to an acquisition or to an appropriation or to a request.

a. Sales

b. Brian Goggin

c. David Drumm

d. Free Education for Everyone

4. _____ or stock market launch is a type of public offering where shares of stock in a company are sold to the general public, on a securities exchange, for the first time. Through this process, a private company transforms into a public company. _____s are used by companies to raise expansion capital, to possibly monetize the investments of early private investors, and to become publicly traded enterprises.

a. Bankmail

b. Bankruptcy costs of debt

c. Bond Tender Offer

d. Initial public offering

5. _____ is the Spanish word for mud brick, a natural building material made from sand, clay, water, and some kind of fibrous or organic material (sticks, straw, and/or manure), usually shaped into bricks using molds and dried in the sun. _____ buildings are similar to cob and rammed earth buildings, but cob and rammed earth are directly made into walls rather than bricks. The Romanian name for this material is chirpici.

a. Adobe

b. Battle of Annaberg

c. Freikorps Lichtschlag

d. Freikorps Oberland

1. d

2. a

3. a

4. d

5. a

You can take the complete Chapter Practice Test

for 19. The Problem of Adverse Selection
on all key terms, persons, places, and concepts.

Online 99 Cents

http://www.JustTheFacts101.com

Use **www.JustTheFacts101.com** for all your study needs

including Facts101's online interactive problem solving labs in

chemistry, statistics, mathematics, and more.

20. The Problem of Moral Hazard

CHAPTER OUTLINE: KEY TERMS, PEOPLE, PLACES, CONCEPTS

_____	Federal Communications Commission
_____	Information asymmetry
_____	Moral hazard
_____	Public offering
_____	Hazard
_____	Insurance
_____	Adverse selection
_____	Google
_____	Cost
_____	Crisis
_____	Financial crisis

CHAPTER HIGHLIGHTS & NOTES: KEY TERMS, PEOPLE, PLACES, CONCEPTS

Federal Communications Commission	The Federal Communications Commission is an independent agency of the United States government, created by Congressional statute to regulate interstate and international communications by radio, television, wire, satellite, and cable in all 50 states, the District of Columbia and U.S. territories. The Federal Communications Commission works towards six goals in the areas of broadband, competition, the spectrum, the media, public safety and homeland security. The Commission is also in the process of modernizing itself.
Information asymmetry	In contract theory and economics, information asymmetry deals with the study of decisions in transactions where one party has more or better information than the other. In contrast to neo-classical economics which assumes perfect information, this is about 'What We Don't Know'. This creates an imbalance of power in transactions which can sometimes cause the transactions to go awry, a kind of market failure in the worst case.

20. The Problem of Moral Hazard

Moral hazard	In economic theory, a moral hazard is a situation where a party will have a tendency to take risks because the costs that could result will not be felt by the party taking the risk. In other words, it is a tendency to be more willing to take a risk, knowing that the potential costs or burdens of taking such risk will be borne, in whole or in part, by others. A moral hazard may occur where the actions of one party may change to the detriment of another after a financial transaction has taken place.
Public offering	A public offering is the offering of securities of a company or a similar corporation to the public. Generally, the securities are to be listed on a stock exchange. In most jurisdictions, a public offering requires the issuing company to publish a prospectus detailing the terms and rights attached to the offered security, as well as information on the company itself and its finances.
Hazard	A hazard is a situation that poses a level of threat to life, health, property, or environment. Most hazards are dormant or potential, with only a theoretical risk of harm; however, once a hazard becomes 'active', it can create an emergency situation. A hazardous situation that has come to pass is called an incident.
Insurance	Insurance is the equitable transfer of the risk of a loss, from one entity to another in exchange for payment. It is a form of risk management primarily used to hedge against the risk of a contingent, uncertain loss. According to study texts of The Chartered Insurance Institute, there are the following categories of risk:•Financial risks which means that the risk must have financial measurement.•Pure risks which means that the risk must be real and not related to gambling•Particular risks which means that these risks are not widespread in their effect, for example such as earthquake risk for the region prone to it. It is commonly accepted that only financial, pure and particular risks are insurable.
Adverse selection	Adverse selection, anti-selection, or negative selection is a term used in economics, insurance, risk management, and statistics. It refers to a market process in which undesired results occur when buyers and sellers have asymmetric information (access to different information); the 'bad' products or services are more likely to be selected. For example, a bank that sets one price for all of its checking account customers runs the risk of being adversely selected against by its low-balance, high-activity (and hence least profitable) customers.
Google	Google is an American multinational corporation specializing in Internet-related services and products. These include search, cloud computing, software, and online advertising technologies. Most of its profits are derived from AdWords.
Cost	In production, research, retail, and accounting, a cost is the value of money that has been used up to produce something, and hence is not available for use anymore. In business, the cost may be one of acquisition, in which case the amount of money expended to acquire it is counted as cost.

20. The Problem of Moral Hazard

Crisis	A crisis is any event that is, or is expected to lead to, an unstable and dangerous situation affecting an individual, group, community, or whole society. Crises are deemed to be negative changes in the security, economic, political, societal, or environmental affairs, especially when they occur abruptly, with little or no warning. More loosely, it is a term meaning 'a testing time' or an 'emergency event'.
Financial crisis	The term financial crisis is applied broadly to a variety of situations in which some financial assets suddenly lose a large part of their nominal value. In the 19th and early 20th centuries, many financial crises were associated with banking panics, and many recessions coincided with these panics. Other situations that are often called financial crises include stock market crashes and the bursting of other financial bubbles, currency crises, and sovereign defaults.

1. _____ is an American multinational corporation specializing in Internet-related services and products. These include search, cloud computing, software, and online advertising technologies. Most of its profits are derived from AdWords.

   a. Google
   b. Blackstartup
   c. Change detection and notification
   d. Chief web officer

2. _____, anti-selection, or negative selection is a term used in economics, insurance, risk management, and statistics. It refers to a market process in which undesired results occur when buyers and sellers have asymmetric information (access to different information); the 'bad' products or services are more likely to be selected. For example, a bank that sets one price for all of its checking account customers runs the risk of being adversely selected against by its low-balance, high-activity (and hence least profitable) customers.

   a. Common Agricultural Policy
   b. Commodity Credit Corporation
   c. Community-supported agriculture
   d. Adverse selection

3. . The term _____ is applied broadly to a variety of situations in which some financial assets suddenly lose a large part of their nominal value. In the 19th and early 20th centuries, many financial crises were associated with banking panics, and many recessions coincided with these panics. Other situations that are often called financial crises include stock market crashes and the bursting of other financial bubbles, currency crises, and sovereign defaults.

   a. Bad bank
   b. Financial crisis

c. Local currency

`d. Demand for money

4. A _____ is the offering of securities of a company or a similar corporation to the public. Generally, the securities are to be listed on a stock exchange. In most jurisdictions, a _____ requires the issuing company to publish a prospectus detailing the terms and rights attached to the offered security, as well as information on the company itself and its finances.

   a. Public offering
   b. Big Bang
   c. Big boy letter
   d. Block trade

5. In contract theory and economics, _____ deals with the study of decisions in transactions where one party has more or better information than the other. In contrast to neo-classical economics which assumes perfect information, this is about 'What We Don't Know'. This creates an imbalance of power in transactions which can sometimes cause the transactions to go awry, a kind of market failure in the worst case.

   a. Credence good
   b. Complexity index
   c. Main effect
   d. Information asymmetry

1. a

2. d

3. b

4. a

5. d

You can take the complete Chapter Practice Test

for 20. The Problem of Moral Hazard
on all key terms, persons, places, and concepts.

Online 99 Cents

http://www.JustTheFacts101.com

Use www.JustTheFacts101.com for all your study needs

including Facts101's online interactive problem solving labs in

chemistry, statistics, mathematics, and more.

21. Getting Employees to Work in the Firm`s Best Interests

_____ Adobe

_____ Agency cost

_____ Agent

_____ Principal

_____ Incentive

_____ Conflict

_____ Decentralization

_____ Sales

_____ Franchising

_____ Moral hazard

_____ Prisoner's dilemma

_____ Problem

_____ Information asymmetry

_____ Free riding

Adobe	Adobe is the Spanish word for mud brick, a natural building material made from sand, clay, water, and some kind of fibrous or organic material (sticks, straw, and/or manure), usually shaped into bricks using molds and dried in the sun. Adobe buildings are similar to cob and rammed earth buildings, but cob and rammed earth are directly made into walls rather than bricks. The Romanian name for this material is chirpici.
Agency cost	An agency cost is an economic concept concerning the cost to a 'principal', when the principal chooses or hires an 'agent' to act on its behalf. Because the two parties have different interests and the agent has more information, the principal cannot directly ensure that its agent is always acting in its (the principal's) best interests. Common examples of this cost include that borne by shareholders (the principal), when corporate management (the agent) buys other companies to expand its power, or spends money on wasteful pet projects, instead of maximizing the value of the corporation's worth; or by the voters of a politician's district (the principal) when the politician (the agent) passes legislation helpful to large contributors to their campaign rather than the voters.
Agent	In economics, an agent is an actor and decision maker in a model. Typically, every agent makes decisions by solving a well- or ill-defined optimization/choice problem. For example, buyers and sellers are two common types of agents in partial equilibrium models of a single market.
Principal	In commercial law, a principal is a person, legal or natural, who authorizes an agent to act to create one or more legal relationships with a third party. This branch of law is called agency and relies on the common law proposition qui facit per alium, facit per se (Latin 'he who acts through another, acts personally'). It is a parallel concept to vicarious liability and strict liability (in which one person is held liable for the acts or omissions of another) in criminal law or torts.
Incentive	An incentive is something that motivates an individual to perform an action. The study of incentive structures is central to the study of all economic activities (both in terms of individual decision-making and in terms of co-operation and competition within a larger institutional structure). Economic analysis, then, of the differences between societies (and between different organizations within a society) largely amounts to characterizing the differences in incentive structures faced by individuals involved in these collective efforts.
Conflict	Conflict refers to some form of friction, disagreement, or discord arising within a group when the beliefs or actions of one or more members of the group are either resisted by or unacceptable to one or more members of another group.

	Conflict can arise between members of the same group, known as intragroup conflict, or it can occur between members of two or more groups, and involve violence, interpersonal discord, and psychological tension, known as intergroup conflict. Conflict in groups often follows a specific course.
Decentralization	Decentralization is the process of redistributing or dispersing functions, powers, people or things away from a central location or authority. While decentralization, especially in the governmental sphere, is widely studied and practiced, there is no common definition or understanding of decentralization. The meaning of decentralization may vary in part because of the different ways it is applied.
Sales	A sale is the act of selling a product or service in return for money or other compensation. Signalling completion of the prospective stage, it is the beginning of an engagement between customer and vendor or the extension of that engagement. The seller or salesperson - the provider of the goods or services - completes a sale in response to an acquisition or to an appropriation or to a request.
Franchising	Franchising is the practice of selling the right to use a firm's successful business model. The word 'franchise' is of Anglo-French derivation - from franc - meaning free, and is used both as a noun and as a (transitive) verb. For the franchisor, the franchise is an alternative to building 'chain stores' to distribute goods that avoids the investments and liability of a chain.
Moral hazard	In economic theory, a moral hazard is a situation where a party will have a tendency to take risks because the costs that could result will not be felt by the party taking the risk. In other words, it is a tendency to be more willing to take a risk, knowing that the potential costs or burdens of taking such risk will be borne, in whole or in part, by others. A moral hazard may occur where the actions of one party may change to the detriment of another after a financial transaction has taken place.
Prisoner's dilemma	The prisoner's dilemma is a canonical example of a game analyzed in game theory that shows why two purely 'rational' individuals might not cooperate, even if it appears that it is in their best interests to do so. It was originally framed by Merrill Flood and Melvin Dresher working at RAND in 1950. Albert W. Tucker formalized the game with prison sentence rewards and gave it the name 'prisoner's dilemma' (Poundstone, 1992), presenting it as follows:Two members of a criminal gang are arrested and imprisoned. Each prisoner is in solitary confinement with no means of speaking to or exchanging messages with the other.
Problem	A problem, which can be caused for different reasons, and, if solvable, can usually be solved in a number of different ways, is defined in a number of different ways. This is determined by the context in which a said problems is defined. When discussed, a problem can be argued in multiple ways.

21. Getting Employees to Work in the Firm`s Best Interests

CHAPTER HIGHLIGHTS & NOTES: KEY TERMS, PEOPLE, PLACES, CONCEPTS

Information asymmetry	In contract theory and economics, information asymmetry deals with the study of decisions in transactions where one party has more or better information than the other. In contrast to neo-classical economics which assumes perfect information, this is about 'What We Don't Know'. This creates an imbalance of power in transactions which can sometimes cause the transactions to go awry, a kind of market failure in the worst case.
Free riding	Free riding is a term used in the stock-trading world to describe the practice of buying shares or other securities without actually having the capital to cover the trade. This is possible when recently bought or sold shares are unsettled, and therefore have not been paid for. Since stock transactions usually settle after three business days, a crafty trader can buy a stock and sell it the following day (or the same day), without ever having sufficient funds in the account.

CHAPTER QUIZ: KEY TERMS, PEOPLE, PLACES, CONCEPTS

1. _____ is the process of redistributing or dispersing functions, powers, people or things away from a central location or authority. While _____, especially in the governmental sphere, is widely studied and practiced, there is no common definition or understanding of _____. The meaning of _____ may vary in part because of the different ways it is applied.

   a. Battlefield promotion
   b. Boundary spanning
   c. Bureaucracy
   d. Decentralization

2. _____ refers to some form of friction, disagreement, or discord arising within a group when the beliefs or actions of one or more members of the group are either resisted by or unacceptable to one or more members of another group. _____ can arise between members of the same group, known as intragroup _____, or it can occur between members of two or more groups, and involve violence, interpersonal discord, and psychological tension, known as intergroup _____. _____ in groups often follows a specific course.

   a. Cigar Box Method
   b. CAPRI model
   c. Conflict
   d. Casa grande

3. . In economic theory, a _____ is a situation where a party will have a tendency to take risks because the costs that could result will not be felt by the party taking the risk.

21. Getting Employees to Work in the Firm`s Best Interests

In other words, it is a tendency to be more willing to take a risk, knowing that the potential costs or burdens of taking such risk will be borne, in whole or in part, by others. A _____ may occur where the actions of one party may change to the detriment of another after a financial transaction has taken place.

a. Credence good
b. Complexity index
c. Moral hazard
d. MANCOVA

4. An _____ is an economic concept concerning the cost to a 'principal', when the principal chooses or hires an 'agent' to act on its behalf. Because the two parties have different interests and the agent has more information, the principal cannot directly ensure that its agent is always acting in its (the principal's) best interests.

Common examples of this cost include that borne by shareholders (the principal), when corporate management (the agent) buys other companies to expand its power, or spends money on wasteful pet projects, instead of maximizing the value of the corporation's worth; or by the voters of a politician's district (the principal) when the politician (the agent) passes legislation helpful to large contributors to their campaign rather than the voters.

a. Complexity index
b. Main effect
c. Agency cost
d. Mixed-design analysis of variance

5. _____ is the Spanish word for mud brick, a natural building material made from sand, clay, water, and some kind of fibrous or organic material (sticks, straw, and/or manure), usually shaped into bricks using molds and dried in the sun. _____ buildings are similar to cob and rammed earth buildings, but cob and rammed earth are directly made into walls rather than bricks. The Romanian name for this material is chirpici.

a. Fuel protests in the United Kingdom
b. Battle of Annaberg
c. Adobe
d. Freikorps Oberland

ANSWER KEY
21. Getting Employees to Work in the Firm`s Best Interests

1. d
2. c
3. c
4. c
5. c

You can take the complete Chapter Practice Test

for 21. Getting Employees to Work in the Firm`s Best Interests
on all key terms, persons, places, and concepts.

Online 99 Cents

http://www.JustTheFacts101.com

Use www.JustTheFacts101.com for all your study needs

including Facts101's online interactive problem solving labs in

chemistry, statistics, mathematics, and more.

CHAPTER OUTLINE: KEY TERMS, PEOPLE, PLACES, CONCEPTS

	Conflict
	Transfer pricing
	Transfer
	Economies of scale
	Learning curve
	Channel stuffing

CHAPTER HIGHLIGHTS & NOTES: KEY TERMS, PEOPLE, PLACES, CONCEPTS

Conflict	Conflict refers to some form of friction, disagreement, or discord arising within a group when the beliefs or actions of one or more members of the group are either resisted by or unacceptable to one or more members of another group. Conflict can arise between members of the same group, known as intragroup conflict, or it can occur between members of two or more groups, and involve violence, interpersonal discord, and psychological tension, known as intergroup conflict. Conflict in groups often follows a specific course.
Transfer pricing	Transfer pricing is a profit allocation method used to attribute a multinational corporation's net profit before tax to countries where it does business. Transfer pricing results in the setting of prices among divisions within an enterprise. Transfer prices are charges for goods and services between controlled (or related) legal entities within an enterprise.
Transfer	As objects of intellectual property or intangible assets, patents and patent applications may be transferred. A transfer of patent or patent application can be the result of a financial transaction, such as an assignment, a merger, a takeover or a demerger, or the result of an operation of law, such as in an inheritance process, or in a bankruptcy. The rationale behind the transferability of patents and patent applications is that it enables inventors to sell their rights and to let other people manage these intellectual property assets both on the valuation and enforcement fronts.

22. Getting Divisions to Work in the Firm's Best Interests

Economies of scale	In microeconomics, economies of scale are the cost advantages that enterprises obtain due to size, output, or scale of operation, with cost per unit of output generally decreasing with increasing scale as fixed costs are spread out over more units of output.
	Often operational efficiency is also greater with increasing scale, leading to lower variable cost as well.
	Economies of scale apply to a variety of organizational and business situations and at various levels, such as a business or manufacturing unit, plant or an entire enterprise.
Learning curve	A learning curve is a graphical representation of the increase of learning with experience (horizontal axis).
	Although the curve for a single subject may be erratic (Fig 1), when a large number of trials are averaged, a smooth curve results, which can be described with a mathematical function (Fig 2). Depending on the metric used for learning (or proficiency) the curve can either rise or fall with experience (Fig 3).
Channel stuffing	Channel stuffing is the business practice where a company, or a sales force within a company, inflates its sales figures by forcing more products through a distribution channel than the channel is capable of selling to the world at large. Also known as 'trade loading', this can be the result of a company attempting to inflate its sales figures. Alternatively, it can be a consequence of a poorly managed sales force attempting to meet short term objectives and quotas in a way that is detrimental to the company in the long term.

1. _____ refers to some form of friction, disagreement, or discord arising within a group when the beliefs or actions of one or more members of the group are either resisted by or unacceptable to one or more members of another group. _____ can arise between members of the same group, known as intragroup _____, or it can occur between members of two or more groups, and involve violence, interpersonal discord, and psychological tension, known as intergroup _____. _____ in groups often follows a specific course.

   a. Cigar Box Method
   b. CAPRI model
   c. Conflict
   d. Casa grande

2. . _____ is a profit allocation method used to attribute a multinational corporation's net profit before tax to countries where it does business. _____ results in the setting of prices among divisions within an enterprise. Transfer prices are charges for goods and services between controlled (or related) legal entities within an enterprise.

   a. Transfer pricing

   b. Controlled foreign corporation

   c. Currency transaction tax

   d. Departure tax

3. As objects of intellectual property or intangible assets, patents and patent applications may be transferred. A _____ of patent or patent application can be the result of a financial transaction, such as an assignment, a merger, a takeover or a demerger, or the result of an operation of law, such as in an inheritance process, or in a bankruptcy.

   The rationale behind the transferability of patents and patent applications is that it enables inventors to sell their rights and to let other people manage these intellectual property assets both on the valuation and enforcement fronts.

   a. Biological patent

   b. Business method patent

   c. Chemical patent

   d. Transfer

4. In microeconomics, _____ are the cost advantages that enterprises obtain due to size, output, or scale of operation, with cost per unit of output generally decreasing with increasing scale as fixed costs are spread out over more units of output.

   Often operational efficiency is also greater with increasing scale, leading to lower variable cost as well.

   _____ apply to a variety of organizational and business situations and at various levels, such as a business or manufacturing unit, plant or an entire enterprise.

   a. Capacity utilization

   b. Economies of scale

   c. Constant elasticity of transformation

   d. Cost-of-production theory of value

5. A _____ is a graphical representation of the increase of learning with experience (horizontal axis).

   Although the curve for a single subject may be erratic (Fig 1), when a large number of trials are averaged, a smooth curve results, which can be described with a mathematical function (Fig 2). Depending on the metric used for learning (or proficiency) the curve can either rise or fall with experience (Fig 3).

   a. Gresham's Law

   b. Learning curve

   c. Constant elasticity of transformation

   d. Cost-of-production theory of value

1. c
2. a
3. d
4. b
5. b

You can take the complete Chapter Practice Test

for 22. Getting Divisions to Work in the Firm`s Best Interests
on all key terms, persons, places, and concepts.

Online 99 Cents

http://www.JustTheFacts101.com

Use www.JustTheFacts101.com for all your study needs

including Facts101's online interactive problem solving labs in

chemistry, statistics, mathematics, and more.

23. Managing Vertical Relationships

	Conflict
	Bundling
	Quality control
	Adobe
	Ping
	Free riding
	Google
	Price discrimination
	Product
	Profit
	Tax avoidance
	Tying
	Antitrust

Conflict	Conflict refers to some form of friction, disagreement, or discord arising within a group when the beliefs or actions of one or more members of the group are either resisted by or unacceptable to one or more members of another group. Conflict can arise between members of the same group, known as intragroup conflict, or it can occur between members of two or more groups, and involve violence, interpersonal discord, and psychological tension, known as intergroup conflict. Conflict in groups often follows a specific course.
Bundling	In political science and public choice theory, bundling is a concept used for studying the selection of candidates for public office. A voter typically chooses a candidate (or party) for the legislature, rather than directly voting for specific policies. When doing so, the voter is essentially selecting among bundles of policies that a candidate or a party will enact if in power.
Quality control	Quality control, or QC for short, is a process by which entities review the quality of all factors involved in production. This approach places an emphasis on three aspects:•Elements such as controls, job management, defined and well managed processes, performance and integrity criteria, and identification of records•Competence, such as knowledge, skills, experience, and qualifications•Soft elements, such as personnel, integrity, confidence, organizational culture, motivation, team spirit, and quality relationships. Controls include product inspection, where every product is examined visually, and often using a stereo microscope for fine detail before the product is sold into the external market. Inspectors will be provided with lists and descriptions of unacceptable product defects such as cracks or surface blemishes for example.
Adobe	Adobe is the Spanish word for mud brick, a natural building material made from sand, clay, water, and some kind of fibrous or organic material (sticks, straw, and/or manure), usually shaped into bricks using molds and dried in the sun. Adobe buildings are similar to cob and rammed earth buildings, but cob and rammed earth are directly made into walls rather than bricks. The Romanian name for this material is chirpici.
Ping	Ping is a computer network administration utility used to test the reachability of a host on an Internet Protocol network and to measure the round-trip time for messages sent from the originating host to a destination computer. The name comes from active sonar terminology which sends a pulse of sound and listens for the echo to detect objects underwater. Ping operates by sending Internet Control Message Protocol (ICMP) echo request packets to the target host and waiting for an ICMP response.
Free riding	Free riding is a term used in the stock-trading world to describe the practice of buying shares or other securities without actually having the capital to cover the trade. This is possible when recently bought or sold shares are unsettled, and therefore have not been paid for.

23. Managing Vertical Relationships

Google	Google is an American multinational corporation specializing in Internet-related services and products. These include search, cloud computing, software, and online advertising technologies. Most of its profits are derived from AdWords.
Price discrimination	Price discrimination or price differentiation is a pricing strategy where identical or largely similar goods or services are transacted at different prices by the same provider in different markets or territories. Price differentiation is distinguished from product differentiation by the more substantial difference in production cost for the differently priced products involved in the latter strategy. Price differentiation essentially relies on the variation in the customers' willingness to pay.
Product	In marketing, a product is anything that can be offered to a market that might satisfy a want or need. In retailing, products are called merchandise. In manufacturing, products are bought as raw materials and sold as finished goods.
Profit	In neoclassical microeconomic theory, the term profit has two related but distinct meanings. Economic profit is similar to accounting profit but smaller because it reflects the total opportunity costs (both explicit and implicit) of a venture to an investor. Normal profit refers to a situation in which the economic profit is zero.
Tax avoidance	Tax avoidance is the legal usage of the tax regime to one's own advantage, to reduce the amount of tax that is payable by means that are within the law. Tax sheltering is very similar, and tax havens are jurisdictions which facilitate reduced taxes. The term tax mitigation is sometimes used; its original use was by tax advisers as an alternative to the pejorative term tax evasion.
Tying	Tying is the practice of selling one product or service as a mandatory addition to the purchase of a different product or service. In legal terms, a tying sale makes the sale of one good (the tying good) to the de facto customer (or de jure customer) conditional on the purchase of a second distinctive good (the tied good). Tying is often illegal when the products are not naturally related.
Antitrust	Competition law is law that promotes or seeks to maintain market competition by regulating anti-competitive conduct by companies. Competition law is known as antitrust law in the United States and anti-monopoly law in China and Russia. In previous years it has been known as trade practices law in the United Kingdom and Australia.

1. _____ is the practice of selling one product or service as a mandatory addition to the purchase of a different product or service. In legal terms, a _____ sale makes the sale of one good (the _____ good) to the de facto customer (or de jure customer) conditional on the purchase of a second distinctive good (the tied good). _____ is often illegal when the products are not naturally related.

   a. Barriers to entry
   b. Bathtub Trust
   c. Tying
   d. Byrd Amendment

2. _____ is an American multinational corporation specializing in Internet-related services and products. These include search, cloud computing, software, and online advertising technologies. Most of its profits are derived from AdWords.

   a. Backlink
   b. Google
   c. Change detection and notification
   d. Chief web officer

3. _____ is the legal usage of the tax regime to one's own advantage, to reduce the amount of tax that is payable by means that are within the law. Tax sheltering is very similar, and tax havens are jurisdictions which facilitate reduced taxes. The term tax mitigation is sometimes used; its original use was by tax advisers as an alternative to the pejorative term tax evasion.

   a. Capital flight
   b. Corlett-Hague rule
   c. Fiscal illusion
   d. Tax avoidance

4. _____ is a term used in the stock-trading world to describe the practice of buying shares or other securities without actually having the capital to cover the trade. This is possible when recently bought or sold shares are unsettled, and therefore have not been paid for.

   Since stock transactions usually settle after three business days, a crafty trader can buy a stock and sell it the following day (or the same day), without ever having sufficient funds in the account.

   a. Free riding
   b. Barbell strategy
   c. BATS Chi-X Europe
   d. Bear raid

5. . _____ refers to some form of friction, disagreement, or discord arising within a group when the beliefs or actions of one or more members of the group are either resisted by or unacceptable to one or more members of another group. _____ can arise between members of the same group, known as intragroup _____, or it can occur between members of two or more groups, and involve violence, interpersonal discord, and psychological tension, known as intergroup _____.

23. Managing Vertical Relationships

_____ in groups often follows a specific course.

a. Cigar Box Method

b. Conflict

c. Cash crop

d. Casa grande

1. c
2. b
3. d
4. a
5. b

You can take the complete Chapter Practice Test

for 23. Managing Vertical Relationships
on all key terms, persons, places, and concepts.

Online 99 Cents

http://www.JustTheFacts101.com

Use www.JustTheFacts101.com for all your study needs

including Facts101's online interactive problem solving labs in

chemistry, statistics, mathematics, and more.

24. You Be the Consultant

CHAPTER OUTLINE: KEY TERMS, PEOPLE, PLACES, CONCEPTS

	Prisoner's dilemma
	Cost
	Utility
	Insurance
	Index

CHAPTER HIGHLIGHTS & NOTES: KEY TERMS, PEOPLE, PLACES, CONCEPTS

Prisoner's dilemma	The prisoner's dilemma is a canonical example of a game analyzed in game theory that shows why two purely 'rational' individuals might not cooperate, even if it appears that it is in their best interests to do so. It was originally framed by Merrill Flood and Melvin Dresher working at RAND in 1950. Albert W. Tucker formalized the game with prison sentence rewards and gave it the name 'prisoner's dilemma' (Poundstone, 1992), presenting it as follows:Two members of a criminal gang are arrested and imprisoned. Each prisoner is in solitary confinement with no means of speaking to or exchanging messages with the other.
Cost	In production, research, retail, and accounting, a cost is the value of money that has been used up to produce something, and hence is not available for use anymore. In business, the cost may be one of acquisition, in which case the amount of money expended to acquire it is counted as cost. In this case, money is the input that is gone in order to acquire the thing.
Utility	Utility is usefulness, the ability of something to satisfy needs or wants. Utility is an important concept in economics and game theory, because it represents satisfaction experienced by the consumer of a good. Not coincidentally, a good is something that satisfies human wants and provides utility, for example, to a consumer making a purchase.
Insurance	Insurance is the equitable transfer of the risk of a loss, from one entity to another in exchange for payment. It is a form of risk management primarily used to hedge against the risk of a contingent, uncertain loss.

24. You Be the Consultant

According to study texts of The Chartered Insurance Institute, there are the following categories of risk:•Financial risks which means that the risk must have financial measurement.•Pure risks which means that the risk must be real and not related to gambling•Particular risks which means that these risks are not widespread in their effect, for example such as earthquake risk for the region prone to it.

It is commonly accepted that only financial, pure and particular risks are insurable.

Index

In economics and finance, an index is a statistical measure of changes in a representative group of individual data points. These data may be derived from any number of sources, including company performance, prices, productivity, and employment. Economic indices (index, plural) track economic health from different perspectives.

1. The _____ is a canonical example of a game analyzed in game theory that shows why two purely 'rational' individuals might not cooperate, even if it appears that it is in their best interests to do so. It was originally framed by Merrill Flood and Melvin Dresher working at RAND in 1950. Albert W. Tucker formalized the game with prison sentence rewards and gave it the name '_____' (Poundstone, 1992), presenting it as follows:Two members of a criminal gang are arrested and imprisoned. Each prisoner is in solitary confinement with no means of speaking to or exchanging messages with the other.

   a. Prisoner's dilemma
   b. Spindletop
   c. Federal Reserve
   d. Libya

2. _____ is usefulness, the ability of something to satisfy needs or wants. _____ is an important concept in economics and game theory, because it represents satisfaction experienced by the consumer of a good. Not coincidentally, a good is something that satisfies human wants and provides _____, for example, to a consumer making a purchase.

   a. Behavioral operations research
   b. Belief decision matrix
   c. Belief structure
   d. Utility

3. . In production, research, retail, and accounting, a _____ is the value of money that has been used up to produce something, and hence is not available for use anymore. In business, the _____ may be one of acquisition, in which case the amount of money expended to acquire it is counted as _____.

In this case, money is the input that is gone in order to acquire the thing.

    a. Cost

    b. Federal Reserve

    c. Fuel protests in the United Kingdom

    d. 2010 student protest in Dublin

4. In economics and finance, an _____ is a statistical measure of changes in a representative group of individual data points. These data may be derived from any number of sources, including company performance, prices, productivity, and employment. Economic indices (_____, plural) track economic health from different perspectives.

    a. Bayesian vector autoregression

    b. Bootstrapping

    c. Censored regression model

    d. Index

5. _____ is the equitable transfer of the risk of a loss, from one entity to another in exchange for payment. It is a form of risk management primarily used to hedge against the risk of a contingent, uncertain loss.

According to study texts of The Chartered _____ Institute, there are the following categories of risk:•Financial risks which means that the risk must have financial measurement.•Pure risks which means that the risk must be real and not related to gambling•Particular risks which means that these risks are not widespread in their effect, for example such as earthquake risk for the region prone to it.

It is commonly accepted that only financial, pure and particular risks are insurable.

    a. Fuel protests in the United Kingdom

    b. Battle of Annaberg

    c. Freikorps Lichtschlag

    d. Insurance

1. a

2. d

3. a

4. d

5. d

You can take the complete Chapter Practice Test

for 24. You Be the Consultant
on all key terms, persons, places, and concepts.

Online 99 Cents

http://www.JustTheFacts101.com

Use www.JustTheFacts101.com for all your study needs

including Facts101's online interactive problem solving labs in

chemistry, statistics, mathematics, and more.